MORE MEMORIES OF
PRESTON

HIGH CLASS
R. Dewhurst
BUTCHER

PILOT
RGK

TRUE NORTH BOOKS
DEAN CLOUGH
HALIFAX
WEST YORKSHIRE HX3 5AX
TEL 01422 344344

073114005

THE PUBLISHERS WOULD LIKE TO THANK THE
FOLLOWING COMPANIES FOR SUPPORTING THE
PRODUCTION OF THIS BOOK

ATTWATER & SONS LIMITED

BAKO NORTH WESTERN LIMITED

RICHARD BAMBER & SON

R BARON LIMITED

E H BOOTH & COMPANY LIMITED

BRITISH AEROSPACE DEFENCE LIMITED

P H CHANDLER (LEYLAND) LIMITED

EDWARD DEWHURST LIMITED

KENT HEALTHCARE

MARLAND BROS LIMITED

JAMES MERCER (PRESTON) LIMITED

CHRIS MILLER (PRESTON) LIMITED

MOORE & SMALLEY

ST PIUS X SCHOOL

PRESTON COLLEGE

PRESTON & SOUTH RIBBLE PARTNERSHIP

T SNAPE & COMPANY LIMITED

TAYLOR PATTERSON ASSOCIATES LIMITED

First published in Great Britain by True North Books
Dean Clough
Halifax, West Yorkshire, HX3 5AX
1998

© TRUE NORTH HOLDINGS

ISBN 1 900 463 17 2

Introduction

The publication of our first book, *Memories of Preston*, met with a tremendous response from the people in the town. Thousands of copies of the original book have been sold to date, with many finding their way overseas to bring pleasure to former Preston residents who had emigrated. The letters of encouragement and kind comments we received urged us to produce a second book, this time containing even more of the excellent photographs which had provided such enjoyment. The compilation of *More Memories of Preston* has been carried out over a period of several months. We always expected it to be a pleasurable experience, but in the event the satisfaction we have derived from studying the marvellous old photographs went far beyond our expectations.

Avenham Park during the 1952 Guild celebrations

Increasingly, *nostalgia* is enjoyed by a growing band of people and the book is intended to appeal to a wide audience. Where possible we have tried to concentrate upon a period within the memory of most of our readers; the 1950s, 60s and 70s - decades which saw tremendous changes in the town, and a time when changes in the world of work, entertainment, public health and retailing. *Change* takes place constantly in every town and Preston is no exception. As we all get older it is often easier to 'step back' and view events and developments with a clearer sense of perspective. Our aim has been to assist in this respect by presenting a 'catalyst' capable of rekindling memories of days gone by in an entertaining manner. Looking through the pages of this book it may be surprising how much change has taken place, and over such a relatively short period, relative to the long history of the area. Several of Preston's best known and longest established firms have allowed us access to their often extensive internal archives. This has enabled us to recount the history of these companies, from humble beginnings to, in most cases, leading positions in their chosen area of expertise. Of course, these organisations have tremendous social, as well as commercial significance, as between them they represent the places of employment for thousands upon thousands of Preston people. We are grateful for the co-operation and support of the directors of these businesses for adding to the quality and interest of this book.

Many different aspects of life in Preston are covered. Home-made entertainment such as the Preston Guild are covered too. Many of the children featured in these photographs will be reaching retirement age now and we would be pleased to hear from anyone who may have recognised themselves.

Street scenes are not neglected. Photographs of this nature were popular in the last book, and understandably so. The changing face of the town is reflected in the way our roads and shops have developed to meet the changing needs of our lives over the years. These photographs show the shops and motorcars we remember from our early days, along with the fashions which were all the rage when we were younger. All combine to refresh our memories of days gone by, and when that occurs the book will have achieved its aim.

We hope that you enjoy reading *More Memories of Preston* as much as we enjoyed compiling it.

PHOTOGRAPH COMPILATION/COVER DESIGN......................................MARK SMITH

CAPTION RESEARCH AND COMPILATION.......................................PEGGY BURNS

DESIGNERS.................MANDY WALKER, NICKY BRIGHTON AND CHRISTINE GALE

COPYWRITER...PAULINE BELL

BUSINESS DEVELOPMENT EDITOR..ANDREW HALES

CONTENTS

Events and occasions

The people of Preston have always loved a good celebration, and the Coronation of King George VI back in 1937 gave them an ideal excuse to really go to town. This fascinating photograph gives us a glance backwards, not just at the riot of Coronation decorations in the town but at the very interesting traffic regulations of the day. Traffic must have presented the Preston authorities with quite a problem even in the days before World War II. Strict regulations were in force, as the rather unusual signs show. Waiting was restricted to one side of the road 'on even dates', and no waiting at all was allowed for longer than thirty minutes at a time. Let's hope that the drivers of the line of cars parked down Lune Street did not take too long over their shopping! The van travelling down the street belonged to Mac Fisheries, who appropriately had a business in Fishergate.

Note the trailer with ladders on the right hand side of the road, and the bike leaning against the wall on the left. What a wonderful sight! It brings back memories of the good old days when you would certainly expect to find the bike and ladders still there on your return.

Above: A sea of thousands of faces: fans wait in Preston's Market Square to greet North End on their return from Wembley in 1937. The lads should have been celebrating victory, as they had been clear favourites in the game against Sunderland. For a while things had looked good, Frank O'Donnell scoring in the 39th minute, giving North End the lead. In the second half however Sunderland began to make up lost ground, going on to score three goals. The trophy was theirs. North End returned home empty handed, but the roars of the fans who were there to welcome the lads home and congratulate them on their remarkable achievement in getting through to Wembley gave the team the encouragement they needed. The 1937 Cup Final was the first ever to be televised.

A year later North End were back at Wembley, this time playing Huddersfield Town. There was no score in the first half, and after ninety minutes of play there was still no score. With only thirty seconds left of the game George Mutch took a penalty. Fans couldn't bear to watch - but with this last kick of extra time Mutch scored the winning goal. Preston North End were home and dry.

Coronation fever hit Preston in 1937 when George VI was crowned king, and a very different Friargate from the road we know today was a riot of red, white and blue. This wonderful old photograph gives us some idea of what the town must have looked like on that memorable occasion. Thick garlands stretched in long lengths from pole to pole while coloured bunting flaps high above the heads of shoppers. Patriotic citizens have hung flags from their windows as the town gears up for its wild party. Meanwhile life went on. An empty shop on the left is being refurbished, perhaps for a new occupant, while further along Speights Ladies Modes tempts shoppers with a display of dresses and hats. Outside the flower shop a step ladder waits for the owner to complete his Coronation decorations. Friargate was not very busy at the time this photograph was taken, and there is little traffic about. In 1937 the motor car was a form of transport that was still largely confined to the middle classes. The ordinary person in the street was more likely to use public transport; a bus bound for Blackpool can be seen heading off up the road.

Above: *An inspection of Preston ex servicemen by their Majesties King George VI and Queen Elizabeth was in progress when this photograph was taken in 1938. Standing tall and straight, the approval of the King and Queen must have done these gallant old soldiers - with those disabled in World War One represented among their number - a power of good. A large crowd turned out, and shop workers forsook their counters to see their popular King and Queen perform the ceremony in the Market Square. Note the sign in the background that reads 'Long may they Reign' - a sentiment echoed by everyone present on that day. War was once more looming on the horizon and King George and Queen Elizabeth with their two beautiful daughters lived and suffered with the people of Britain through the dark days of war. The king and queen showed great courage by staying on in England when they could have been evacuated to safety. They insisted that they be treated like everyone else, even to wartime rationing, and the King was almost relieved when Buckingham Palace was bombed. He felt that he could now identify with his people and look them in the face.*

Left: *The town of Preston was plunged into mourning by the death of their much loved King George V in 1936, and hundreds of his devoted subjects turned out on that cold January day to pay their respects and show their loyalty to their sovereign. George Duke of York came to the throne in 1910. The model of the ideal Englishman, King George had made himself immensely popular with his subjects without really trying. He was tolerant of people whose opinions differed from his own - but not afraid to speak his mind when the occasion called for straight talking. Dignified, fair, conscientious and modest, he once remarked on the warmth with which people greeted him on his Silver Jubilee in 1935, 'I am beginning to think they like me for myself.' George V was the first monarch to broadcast the Christmas Day message which over the years became the established tradition that we still enjoy today. Now King George was dead, and even the heavily draped pillars were in mourning in Preston at his memorial service. This photograph was taken during the two minutes' silence that marked his people's respect on this solemn occasion. The King's widow, Queen Mary, lived on until 1953.*

Above: Some older Prestonians will no doubt remember the occasion when this atmospheric photograph of a demonstration of air raid precautions was taken in 1938. War was looking inevitable, and for the first time in history bomber aircraft were capable of carrying bombs over long distances, so the citizens of Britain faced a very real threat from the air. On the 15th March a meeting was held in the Guild Hall in Preston. After the meeting, demonstrations of emergency procedures were given in the market place, and young and old learned how best to protect themselves and their families in the even of an air raid. In World War One mustard gas had been used with deadly effect by Germany, and it was widely expected that they would employ the use of gas again. Note the sign that warns 'Danger Mustard Gas' in the top right hand corner of the photograph, and the two rubber-suited workers who would be expected to deal with any major attack. A young boy, photographed by a press photographer for posterity, helps out with the demonstration. One might wonder where the boy is now, and what he did with his life.

Right: Bunting flies gaily above allotments in Preston on this red letter day in 1945. It is the 18th June to be precise, and the cheerful bunch of lads in the photograph are the Holme Slack Boys. Their hard work with spade and hoe has been recognised by the Mayor and Mayoress themselves, who have just completed their inspection of the fine produce displayed in the centre of the photograph, and the allotments where the lads grew it all. Cabbage, turnips, broad beans, lettuce and salad stuff and even flowers - it's all there, and all produced by the youngsters themselves, who deserved every bit of the praise they were given.

World War II had just ended, and Britain was still feeling the pinch. All through the war, the government encouraged people to 'dig for victory', and in the neat front gardens of the land roses were replaced by cabbages and delphiniums were dug out to make way for the humble potato. In a land where food was strictly rationed and dried eggs were used for cooking, hen runs became popular with many people, while those who could manage it even kept a pig or two.

Above: This photograph was taken on 7th March 1945, and another Royal Visit encourages the loyal citizens of Preston to hang on for just a while longer. There are some happy, smiling faces in the crowd, and a few sad ones. Though the town fared better than many during the war, each person had his or her story to tell, some of personal tragedy, many of amazing fortitude in hard times. But the light at the end of Britain's long dark tunnel was growing brighter. Two months after this visit of the King and Queen to Preston Adolf Hitler had departed this life to face his Maker, committing suicide in his Berlin bunker. On 7th May 1945 Germany surrendered unconditionally, bringing the war in Europe to an end.

The troops were tired. The people were tired. Even the buildings in this photograph look tired. But the war was over, and the citizens of Preston, along with the rest of Britain, found the energy to let down their hair. They simply went wild with joy, and on 13th May 1945 they lined the streets of the town in their hundreds to hear the band play and watch the Victory Parade march past. Here, those who returned safely march along a vastly different Lancaster Road from the one we are familiar with today. Older Prestonians will remember this corner of Lancaster and Lord Street, and the Derby Arms just around the corner. All were swept away in the late 1960s to make way for the brand new Guild Hall. The diggers moved on to the site on 17th July 1970 and the new building opened almost exactly three years later. The unusual octagonal building was controversial from the first; some love it, some hate it - but nobody ignores it! Looked on by many as outstanding architecture of national importance, to others the building, despite its rather grand civic entrance, became the 'Terrible Toadstool' or the 'Preston Pomegranate'.

Above: The war was over, and things were back on track as England went forward towards the 1950s. The cotton trade was in full swing and on the 13th September 1945 the Minister of Labour, Mr Isaacs himself, paid a visit to Horrockses, Crewdson & Company. The photograph shows Mr H H Mallett on the left with the Mayor on the right of the photograph, while Mr Isaacs closely examines the work that this young girl is producing on her Jones sewing machine. Her name unfortunately does not seem to have been recorded. Horrockses Crewdsons mill was founded by John Horrocks in 1791, which, considering that John had no personal funds to work with, and that he was only 23 at the time, was a remarkable achievement. The mock medieval building in Stanley Street with its entrance lodge and large clock, became a familiar sight. In his short life Horrocks founded no fewer than seven cotton mills in Preston, encouraged by inventions like Richard Arkwright's water frame. Arkwright himself was the youngest child of a poor Preston family. His water frame made him a rich man and when he died in 1792 he left a fortune of half a million pounds.

Right: A pilot police car heads up the royal procession as a stately line of limousines cruises past the cheering crowds. The people of Preston turned out in their thousands on this sunny day to catch a glimpse of King George VI, the Queen and Princess Margaret when they visited Preston in 1951.
A royal visit was all too rare an event, and one can feel the excitement of the people lining the roadside in this wonderful old photograph. Children crowd to the front and parents hold small toddlers high to see the royal family for the very first time, while those unfortunates at the back of the crowd temporarily abandon their luckless babies and crane their necks for a better view. A good natured police officer gently persuades people not to get run over in their eagerness to get as close as they can to the royal cars. One wonders whether the staff of the fish and chip shop further down the road were actually outside watching the parade or slaving over the proverbial hot stove, cooking up mountains of Britain's favourite take away food in the expectation of record takings!

Below: The year was 1945. The war was over, and Britain went wild with joy as the news that everybody was waiting for was announced. It was good to be alive, and thousands of Prestonians turned out to watch the victory parade held on 13th May, here seen passing the Town Hall. Britain was far from being out of the woods, however. A general election was held on 5 July, resulting in a landslide victory for Labour. The new Prime Minister, Clement Attlee, warned that though there was peace, there was no likelihood of prosperity in the immediate future. With countries decimated by war there was a worldwide food shortage, and there was to be no let up in the food rationing that Britain had grown used to during the war. In fact a year later in 1946 bread went on ration, though the first bananas that had been seen since before the war arrived from the West Indies. Children born during the war had never seen a banana before, and had no idea how to eat them! Clothes rationing ended in 1949, but it was not until 1954 that all rationing ended in Britain.

Right: This stunning photograph of little girls dancing around a maypole was taken during the Guild celebrations of 1952. Their maypole is a simple affair: just a broom handle, a few lengths of wire, some garlands and a few coloured ribbons. But some caring adult has put all the ingredients together with artistic skill so that the children can play their part in the festival and have a marvellous time. Dancing round the maypole is a very ancient tradition, but in many parts of Lancashire, as recently as the 1940s, groups of little girls would carry their beautifully decorated, home made miniature maypoles from house to house on May Day, the 1st May, every year. They would dance around their 'May Queen', who would sit on a little stool in the centre, and sing a special song as their ribbons entwined. The neighbour would watch their little show and spare the girls a few coppers - then off the children would go to the next house to do it all again.

Below: It was yet another red letter day in the life of Preston when the Queen visited the town in 1955. The town has been privileged to have many royal visits over the years, but loyal citizens have never failed to turn out in their hundreds to show their love and respect to their sovereign. Great crowds were waiting at the station to see their elegant and beautiful young Queen, and many more lined the streets outside to catch a glimpse of her and raise a resounding cheer as she passed by. Queen Elizabeth I had been queen for a matter of three years or so when this photograph was taken. She is here seen being greeted as she left the train at Preston Railway Station; she was welcomed to the town by the Mayor and Aldermen and other dignitaries. Her husband the Duke of Edinburgh was with her, looking young, tall and handsome - he can be seen in the background, to the left of the photograph.

Right: The year was 1953 and a touch of gaiety brings a lively sparkle to the usually austere surroundings as the workforce at Leigh's Mill take the opportunity to do the old place proud in readiness for the Coronation of Queen Elizabeth I. Patriotic flags and coloured streamers are strung across the room, while red, white and blue ribbons encircle the building's supporting pillars. Even the light shades in their frivolous skirts join in the fun. The workers appear to be enjoying themselves, as the wide and genuine smiles on most of these ladies' faces show. Their cheerful flowered aprons, typical workwear of the time, add their own touch to the happy occasion. A few of them would perhaps get to watch the crowning of the Queen in Westminster Abbey on television - the first time a Coronation has ever been filmed. Though Britain had a television service as early as 1936, few people could afford to buy the expensive sets. By the 1950s they were beginning to get cheaper, and the Queen's Coronation presented many families with the ideal reason to buy or rent a TV set. Those who did not simply crowded into the parlours of more fortunate neighbours to watch the event!

Above: Envied by many of their male contemporaries, Brian London and a rather boyish Michael Parkinson performed the extremely pleasant task of judging the Miss Presston title back in 1965, and were rewarded for their efforts by having a couple of the lovely ladies sit on their knees. No doubt it was not easy to choose from the many hopeful entrants but in the end Pat Finch, on the left of the photograph, went home with the title. More than thirty years on it is very interesting to view 'Parky' in this very different role. We tend to forget that long before he was King of the chat show he was himself a journalist. He carried on his career in journalism with Granada Television, working with news magazines such as 'What the Papers Say', 'Cinema' and, of course, 'World in Action'. In the end, though, it was his memorable role as the host of 'Parkinson' for which he will be remembered. After all, who can forget the night he battled for his dignity against Emu and Rod Hull? Michael Parkinson delighted audiences with his regular Saturday evening chat show throughout the 1970s, and the show was an audience puller for eleven years.

Right: Getting a taste of the real thing - the cast of the TV series 'Z-Cars' test out the equipment at County Police Headquarters on a visit in May 1964.
The long running police drama series strangely enough owed its origins to a bout of mumps. To pass the time Troy Kennedy Martin, confined to bed and feeling very fed up with life, tuned in to the police waveband, and discovered a whole new world that was nothing like the comfy 'Dixon of Dock Green' type of policing portrayed on television. He took up a pen and began to write, and the result was a completely different type of police drama that even had a nasty and aggressive superior officer, Charlie Barlow, played by Stratford Johns. In fact Martin's characters were all fallible human beings who had their own personal vices such as gambling and drinking. The series, that portrayed the real relationship between police and the community, kicked off in 1962 on BBC 1 and immediately gained a huge following. In 1965 Watt and Barlow were given their own series 'Softly, Softly', but 'Z-Cars' returned to our screens between 1967 and 1978 with new blood to replace them.

Above: Much bravery was shown by dock workers the day that fire broke out at a warehouse used by Northern Ireland Trailers. When a small fire started among cases being unloaded, men at first tackled the blaze themselves with extinguishers and hosepipes. But soon it was clear that professional help was needed. Four fire engines, including a turntable ladder, dashed to the site which was already well alight, fed by 1,000 bales of Acrilan fibre stored there. One of the workers, Brian Brundle, suffered burns as he drove a tanker to safety. He was only one of the heroes of the day; several braved the flames to rescue vital documents from the office, while others ran to push cars away. Eventually the intense heat, exploding asbestos and thick smoke drove them back.

With a strong wind whipping the flames into a fury, the building was doomed. Firefighters, showered with asbestos particles, concentrated on preventing the fire from reaching nearby kerosene tanks. An explosion among them would have been a major incident, with people killed and the docks destroyed. Seven ambulances stood by but only two men needed hospital treatment. The thick pall of black smoke could be seen for many miles.

Around the town centre

Flags fly high, colourful bunting snaps in the breeze, and miles of red, white and blue garlands swing from every available telegraph pole and lamp post. The year was 1937, and the entire town of Preston was in party mood ready for the Coronation of King George VI. Some older Prestonians will still be able to remember Church Street as it was in this photograph, and perhaps even recall Roger Pickup's, the grocer's shop on the right of the photograph. The advertisements on the wall for Libby's milk and Capstan cigarettes will strike a chord, though today's more enlightened approach to the dangers of smoking has brought with it much more low key advertising. The general sadness that had followed the death in 1936 of the much loved and respected George V had been slow to dissipate, but Britain had wholeheartedly welcomed his elder son King Edward VIII. The popular king had reigned for only a few months, however, before he abdicated without being crowned. His younger brother took up the reigns as King George VI. The country was in the mood for a Coronation, and they welcomed their shy new king with open hearts.

Above: *The Grand Junction Hotel, on the corner near the zebra crossing, cannot be seen clearly in this photograph that dates back to August 1953. But the pub that gave its identity to the Grand Junction Roundabout was believed to be older than the surrounding streets of houses, and was already serving the people of Preston when the docks were opened in 1892 - the year that the Wheatsheaf, the pub that can be seen on the roundabout, was opened. Watery Lane was hung with bunting on the day that Prince Albert, the Duke of Edinburgh (Queen Victoria's second son) visited the town to officially declare Preston Docks open. A huge sign that read 'Welcome Sailor Prince' spanned the road right outside the Grand Junction. Huge crowds were waiting to welcome the prince. Church bells rang and schoolchildren in white sang as the royal visitor travelled to the docks. The steam yacht 'Aline' was the first vessel to enter the brand new dock, though few facilities had yet been installed when the docks were opened on Saturday 25th June. The docks that came in with a bang sadly went out like a damp squib in the early 1980s.*

Below: *Where did they all go to? Police officers on point duty, that is. There was a time when every major junction in every major town had its traffic cop; remember those black and white zebra-striped boxes they used to use? The boxes made them highly visible and gave them the elevation and air of authority they needed. Point duty must have demanded a high concentration of manpower, however, and it was no doubt argued that instead of directing the town's traffic the Lancashire Constabulary would be better employed in concentrating their force on the fight against crime. So a few at a time they departed, leaving the motorist with a legacy of traffic lights to contend with at each junction. Traffic lights, while no doubt keeping the traffic flowing smoothly through the town centre, somehow lack the personal touch provided by the good old British bobby. The junction of Corporation Street and Fishergate, though controlled now of course by sets of traffic lights, has changed little from the time this photograph was taken. The buildings are still there, though of course the companies using them have since changed.*

Below: This dramatic aerial photograph was taken looking south from an altitude of 2000 feet. North Road is the main route running diagonally from the top left to the bottom right of the picture. The retail heart of Preston can be seen at the top of the photograph, with Fishergate running from right to left, and the best known high street shops following the same course. The dark outline of the Parish Church can be made out to the left of Fishergate. Just above and to the left of the centre of the photograph the old bus station is in view. Land cleared nearer to the direction of the camera would later be the site of the new bus station, and the route of the much-needed inner relief road would pass over the area shown lower down this picture. The picture captures a moment in the development of Preston when a tremendous amount of development work was under way. The best evidence of this is shown in the form of the St. George's Shopping Centre, opened in 1966 and greatly improved in 1981. The Fishergate Centre, a friendly rival to St. George's, would not appear until the early 1980s when it would occupy a prominent position at the top right of this picture.

Right: An almost three-dimensional effect is created by the photographer responsible for this aerial scene. Lancaster Road runs upwards from the bottom left of the picture and on the right hand side Cheapside can be seen leading to Market Street and Friargate. Traversing the photograph, from left to right and three-quarters of the way up it, is Fishergate. The parish Church is clearly visible in this area as is another building virtually in the centre, Crystal House, with its distinctive modern concrete and glass design. Another distinctive shape, and one which most Prestonians would declare more affection for, is that of the Harris Museum. The top right of the photograph affords a tiny section of the River Ribble to be seen, with Winkley Square a few hundred yards below it. Back to the centre of the photograph, and the bustling markets area is shown above the tightly-packed streets and buildings that characterised this part of Preston for decades. The new road system would transform much of the foreground in this picture when it was constructed to ease the growing congestion in the inner area.

The heavy traffic and the number of pedestrians and shoppers suggests that this photograph might have been taken on a Saturday, the big shopping day in Preston in the 1950s. Lune Street had long been at the heart of Preston's shopping area, and a number of the businesses in the street had traded there for many years. The 1950s saw many changes in Britain's shopping habits. The Festival of Britain in 1951 kicked off the new decade, infusing the country with a spirit of new hope, and in 1954 all rationing in Britain was ended, bringing to an end the last of wartime belt tightening restrictions. Brand names once more appeared on certain food products, and young people were amazed to realise that products such as margarine could be labelled as Stork or Summer County instead of just being plain old foul tasting margarine. The end of the decade saw the rise of the self service store. The trend started slowly, but it was the thin end of the wedge. Over the last forty or so years there has been a shift towards super- and hyper-markets and out of town shopping.

After the usual series of unexpected hitches and panics the event got underway - and of course turned out to be a resounding success that was talked about not for weeks or months, but for many years to come. The next Guild Merchant is planned for the year 2012.

Top: Is it a bird? Is is a plane? If it's labelled 'Babcock and Wilcox', chances are that this leviathan toiling along London Road in Walton le Dale has something to do with boilers; with 130 years of experience behind them, the name Babcock and Wilcox has become synonymous with the word 'boilers'. It was back in 1856 that Stephen Wilcox invented the first safety water tube boiler; its forerunner, the 'fire tube' design, often exploded, killing and injuring workers. Eleven years on he went into partnership with George Babcock to make and market the invention. Thomas Edison hailed the invention as 'the best boiler God has permitted man yet to make.' In the late 1940s a shop assembled backage boiler was developed that could be shipped to the customer and installed on site. Perhaps the subject of this wonderful old photograph, which probably dates back to the early 1960s, is one of them. Interestingly, in 1997 George Babcock and Stephen Wilcox were inducted into the National Inventors Hall of Fame in Ohio for their contribution to industry. Cyclists were only too pleased to vacate the road and keep well out of the way as this terrifying monster roared past them.

Above: This photograph could be dubbed the calm before the storm, or perhaps more correctly, the drawing of breath before the all out effort. Guild celebrations for 1952 were about to get underway, and Preston had not seen preparations like this since 1922 - a 30 year gap had been left instead of the usual 20, as of course Britain had been at war in 1942, when the Guild Merchant should have been held. The entire town threw itself into a frenzy of preparation. Events were discussed and devised, exhibitions were planned and individual exhibits prepared. Sewing machines across the town hummed busily as the costumes for the many processions, dancing displays and shows were cut out, tacked together, fitted on and run up. Lines were memorised, songs practised and dozens of tableaux planned, constructed and decorated.

Preston has long been a town with a large Catholic population, and the Roman Catholic Procession has always been one of the key features of the Guild Celebrations. This delightful photograph from 1952 shows a group of school-children leading the churches' procession into the Market Square from Friargate, the girls charmingly dressed in white, the boys smart in shirts and dark shorts. In the foreground, two young boys fittingly carry the cross that symbolises the Christian message behind each of the tableaux that follow. As usual a huge crowd had gathered, and many of them were fortunate enough to be able to find a seat as they reverently watched the procession make its way past. The right to hold a Guild Merchant at twenty year intervals was granted by charter from Henry II as long ago as 1179. In those far off days the celebrations and feasting went on for a staggering six weeks!

Right: Many older Prestonians will remember Lune Street as it was in 1958, perhaps with a tinge of regret - though St George's Shopping Centre, opened in 1964, serves the town well, and Ringway, which replaced much of this busy shopping area, fulfils its purpose in keeping town centre traffic moving. Remember the Corporation Arms? And the Old Spread Eagle? The Eagle was opened in 1802 when Lune Street was built, and took its licence from 'Matty's Whim', an old inn that dates back to the 1700s and once stood nearby in the passage that led to St George's Church. Lune Street had a host of shops and services to offer Preston: you could buy a piano or a radio at Crane & Sons, have your hair done at Smith's or Marjorie's, buy your Sunday joint of meat at Dewhurst and furnish your home at the nearby Harrops store. You could have your eyes tested and your teeth filled, insure your house, divorce your spouse, have a suit made and publish a book, all within the space of a hundred yards or so.

Left: Remember Lancaster Road when it looked like this? There was a sale on at Fryer and Hancock when this photograph was taken in 1964. The buildings to the left of the Ribble Motor Services (the single storey white building) had only a few more years left to them at this time, and by 1970 the row of properties had been demolished and bulldozers had moved in to clear the site for the new Guild Hall. The grand civic entrance to the striking octagonal building we know today is quite different from anything else in Preston. The new premises provided the town with a 2,000 seat concert hall, and though the building had its critics, most Prestonians today feel quite comfortable with the Guild Hall. The original Guild Hall had once been part of the Town Hall which, after managing to survive World War Two unscathed, burnt down in 1947. After the fire, two models were made of the Town Hall's spire from timber taken from the Guild Hall. Parchment scrolls were placed inside the models, which were sent on a round the world journey. Former citizens of Preston who lived on the route taken by the models were invited to sign the scrolls.

Below: Sandbags protect the august pillars of Preston Town Hall from aerial attack in this 1939 photograph. During the years that followed the Great War, long range bombers had been developed, which meant that the Second World War was the first war that held any real threat from the air. Both Britain and Germany now possessed aircraft which were capable of carrying large bomb loads and flying for long distances. People were not sure of what they could expect from this new and untried method of waging war, but they took the sensible view of preparing for the worst while hoping for the best. Important buildings were protected by sandbags; citizens were taught how to defend themselves in the event of an air raid, and every man, woman and child carried their gas mask around with them in case Germany should resort once more to the use of mustard gas. The uniformed lady in the photograph has hers safely over shoulder.

In 1938 Adolf Hitler signed the Munich Agreement and Britain's Prime Minister, Neville Chamberlain, made the mistake of trusting him. Many, however, did not, and by 1939 war had broken out. The citizens of Great Britain drew breath and prepared themselves for another long siege.

Right: Drawn by the drama of the moment, crowds gather to watch the sad end of one of Preston's favourite stores. It was 12th March 1965 when fire broke out at Goobys. Fire trucks were quickly on the scene. Firefighters battled to save the blazing building, then as it became clear that Goobys was doomed, concentrated on the fight to prevent fire from spreading to nearby properties. The photograph captures the sadness of the event: fire hoses snake about the wet road, firefighters battle with the blaze from the tops of long ladders, smoke billows across the roof, and the empty windows of the smoke blackened store front emphasise the untimely death of Goobys.

The store started life as an exclusive ladies' milliner, and Goobys was known as the place to buy a hat for that grand occasion. Later, it became known for carrying the latest fashions, and served by shop assistants dressed in smart and sober black, ladies could buy an entire outfit at Goobys.

Other old properties in Church Street were also doomed. Even the well loved old Empire, by this time a bingo hall, was swept away to make room for the modern shopping development that stands there today.

Left: A rare eagle's eye view of Preston town centre that gives us a chance to compare styles of architecture across the years - and Preston is a town that has seen many changes. The year is 1972, and stands are already in place for that year's Guild Merchant processions. The magnificent Harris Library building with its pillared entrance leaps out of the picture, as does Crystal House, in the bottom right of the photograph. Crystal House was planned after the splendid old Town Hall, which stood nearby, burnt down in 1947. The block (what else can you call it?) was designed as 'A showpiece shop and office block' and its construction was completed in 1964. Many Prestonians were dismayed that the alien building looked so out of place in situ, against so many old and beautiful buildings. The new Guild Hall, at the top right hand side, though different, has now become accepted; opinions have softened over the years as it has earned its place in the community. Since this photograph was taken St George's Shopping Centre has been developed, covered in, and has taken over the area at the bottom left of the photograph. Further extensions to the centre are planned.

Above: The people of Preston enjoy an evening's entertainment as much as the next person, and this was as true at the turn of the Twentieth Century as it is today. The Hippodrome, boasting a typically Victorian and rather elegant cast iron arcade around the entrance, opened its doors in Friargate on Monday 16th January 1905. The facility quickly established itself as a favourite venue for a night out among the theatre going citizens of Preston.

Over the years the town has had many theatres and cinemas: the Empire Theatre, which was opened in 1911; the Theatre Royal, the short-lived ABC Cinema, to name only a few. All came to a sad and inglorious end. The Theatre Royal was demolished. The Hippodrome gave way to the redeveloper and was swept away in 1959 to make way for C & A Modes. The Empire Theatre succumbed to the rise in popularity of television that started during the late 1950s, and when the establishment began to suffer from dwindling audiences it was converted into a bingo hall - the fate of many once popular cinemas of the time.

At leisure

Below: 1954, and Preston North End were FA Cup finalists again. The contest was a real nail biter. Twenty minutes into the game Ronnie Allen, the West Brom centre-forward, put his team into the lead - but one minute later Angus Morrison brought the scores level. North End took the lead in the second half, but Allen went on to score for Albion. North End were very unlucky not to lift the trophy; a cross-shot by Griffin got past North End's keeper George Thompson. The losers' medal went to North End Captain Tom Finney. Tom Finney signed as a professional footballer in 1940, quickly proving that he was a world class player. Always the complete gentleman footballer, Sir Tom Finney was tough but not rough, assertive but not aggressive. A player of incredible skill, he was twice named Footballer of the Year (the first player to gain this honour twice). He played in a total of 433 league games, netting 187 goals on his way, and played 40 FA Cup games, scoring 23 goals. He was awarded the OBE in 1961, the CBE in 1992, and in the 1998 New Years Honours List was declared a knight of the realm.

Facing page, bottom: This very old photograph of Moore's Regatta Inn dates back to 1914, the first year of World War One. The inn itself was very old, and in the 18th and 19th centuries it was known as the Little Bridge Inn, a name that referred to the original ancient stone bridge (Fishergate Lane) which incidentally still survives below the south side of Fishergate Hill. The Regatta Inn, which was situated at the junction of Fishergate Hill and Strand Road, was demolished to make way for construction of the new bridge over the River Syke. Interestingly, the River Syke once drove Richard Arkwright's water frame, invented in 1768. The machine used rollers to stretch the cotton threads, producing very strong yarn. The 18th Century saw many key inventions, but the water frame could be said to be the main factor in the onset of the modern factory age. Richard Arkwright came from a poor Preston family and had very little education (in his 50s he spent two hours a day studying grammar and spelling). He did not allow his lack of formal education to hold him back, however; Arkwright was the first cotton magnate in English history.

Above: Celebrating the fact that their team were good enough to have got to Wembley, even if they had come home minus the coveted cup, crowds of fans welcome their team home after their 2-3 defeat to West Ham in 1964. Howard Kendall, second from the end on the right of the photograph, was at the age of 17 the youngest player ever to appear in a Cup Final. (Since then his record has been broken by Paul Allen who played for West Ham United.) It was a classic final. Kendall started out by playing for England Schoolboys, and once he had been spotted, he quickly proved his worth, scoring his first League goal when Preston beat Southampton 5-4. Under Alf Ramsey, Kendall was chosen for an FA team to play two matches in Gibraltar. He was a good choice; the side won both games, and Kendall scored in each one. Preston North End Football Club have a long history, and their first football match was played around 1878. Subscriptions at that time were twopence a week!

In the large natural amphitheatre of Avenham Park, framed by a background of stately trees and greenery, the Merrie England performance attracted large crowds of music lovers to this popular part of the 1952 Guild Celebration, when Preston Cecilian Choral Society and the Preston Guild Drama Club performed Sir Edward German's light opera. The weather appears to have treated the players and their audience kindly on the day of this particular concert, though as the performance was repeated twice more we have to hope that this remained the case. The Guild Merchant has been held for centuries, and music has always played a very important part in the celebrations. In this 1952 Guild, bands played lively marches for the many processions, there was open air dancing every night and the rather special Carnival Dance was eagerly looked forward to by many toe tapping nimble footed citizens of Preston.

Above: *Proud parents and grandparents were among the hundreds of admiring spectators who crowded into Avenham Park to watch the Guild Festival for Schools in 1952. The subject of this particular display has long been forgotten except perhaps by a handful of adults who took part in the Festival long ago when they were children. We can gather from this atmospheric photograph, however, that groups of young boys dressed in extravagant and colourful costume proudly played their part for their mums and dads, while just for the day 70 or so little girls were fairies, all dressed in white with gauzy wings spread, and performed their dance in an almost perfect circle. Pure magic. The Preston Guild Merchant has often been referred to as 'England's greatest carnival.' Be that as it may, the celebrations brought together the town's schools, churches, industries, and sporting and hobbies enthusiasts in a way that nothing else could.*

Above: The year was 1937 and on the day this photograph was taken a military parade was expected in Moor Park, Preston's largest open space. The occasion was the Coronation of King George VI, and a large crowd of spectators of all ages had gathered to join in the fun.

Albert, Duke of York, had been hurled unexpectedly into the kingship he had not been trained for when his older brother Edward VIII, who had been king for a mere 325 days, renounced the throne on 10 December 1936 for American divorcee Wallis Simpson, 'the woman I love.' The new king was shy and nervous and suffered from an embarrassing stammer (which he later overcame with medical aid and the support of his wife Queen Elizabeth). 'I'm only a naval officer,' he confessed to his cousin Lord Louis Mountbatten on the day he became king. 'It's the only thing I know about.' He had never seen a state paper in his life. But he rose to the challenge, squared his shoulders, and adopted the title of George VI. King George VI went on to take his place as perhaps Britain's most well loved monarch. The bunting flaps gaily in the breeze as hungry diners make their way across the forecourt in front of Binfields Cafe in Watling Street Road. The photograph dates back to 1952, which gives us a clue to the reason for the bunting. 1952 was of course a Guild Merchant year, and Binfields were celebrating along with everyone else in town. Preston must have been a wonderful sight.

Below: The painted church on the banner is echoed by the spire of the same church in this charming photograph taken in 1952. Members of what is thought to be Fulwood Wesleyan Church are about to join the Preston Guild Free Churches procession. Pretty girls in light summery dresses hold on daintily to the strings while a couple of burly blokes put their backs into the heavy stuff and prepare to carry the banner around the streets of Preston. Interestingly, one can estimate the ages of some of the girls in the picture by the details of their dress. The ones wearing white ankle socks would have been 13 or under, as girls were not judged old enough to wear stockings until they were 14 or 15. Pairs of light gloves, the adjunct to every well dressed, church-going young lady's costume, completed their elegant outfits. Nice work, Miss Marple.

Many of the scores of beautiful banners used in the processions and the many exhibitions that were staged were the work of local Preston artists.

Above: The bunting flaps gaily in the breeze as hungry diners make their way across the forecourt in front of Binfields Cafe in Watling Street Road. The photograph dates back to 1952, which gives us a clue to the reason for the bunting. 1952 was of course a Guild Merchant year, and Binfields were celebrating along with everyone else in town. Preston must have been a wonderful sight. A sign outside the cafe advertises 'high teas', but confusingly reads 'The Broadway Cafe', leaving us to wonder whether the sign had been left there by a previous owner.

Binfields were confectioners as well as offering teas and snacks, and their tempting cakes and pastries made them well known in the area. Watling Street Road was largely a residential area, but the road had its full complement of shops - grocers, butchers, a Coop and The Barracks electricity and hardware store were a few of the local shops that offered an all round service to the local area. Note the bicycle rack outside the cafe; cycling has long been a 'green' way to get around Preston. Preston has its hills, but there are hillier places in the UK.

On the move

Below: Hopelessly lost and oblivious to the needs of other road users, a driver and his wife obstruct the traffic and park their little convertible almost in the middle of the road while they discuss (or argue about?) the route they need to take to get where they need to be. We might suggest that they should begin by consulting the Highway Code rather than a road map. Other less involved parties might suggest a couple of rather neat solutions to their problem. The most obvious is of course to carry on to the top of the road, where they can read the prominent signpost which is quite likely to give them a clue as to what direction they should take. The other solution is the more pleasant; they should park their car thoughtfully in the pub car park and withdraw to the Saddle Inn, where the young lady could soothe her ruffled nerves with a half of Wilkins while her husband drowns his sorrows in lemonade. Can anyone, without running the risk of being labelled 'sexist' (heaven forbid!) read any significance into the fact that it is the man who is doing the driving?

A surprising number of people never knew that Preston had docks - probably because the situation of the town, so far up the river Ribble, made it seem unlikely. But so it had, and they were quite large docks, too, that not only handled imports and exports but supported a ferry service between Preston and Ireland. Preston docks played an important part in the life of the town, and contributed much over the years to the success of Lancashire's trade and industry.

The exact date of this evocative photograph is unfortunately unknown, though perhaps it was taken during the 1940s or 50s. The picture shows Columbian pine being discharged in Albert Edward Dock. Huge derricks aboard the vessel are ready with block and tackle to lower timber on to the dock. Stevedores working on the dockside are dwarfed by the huge stacks of sawn timber already offloaded from the ship. Another rather smaller vessel lies behind, perhaps a coaster.

Today Riversway, the redevelopment of Preston's former docks, offers a host of leisure facilities, with shops, a UCI cinema, a marina, and accommodation - and as an added attraction the tall ship 'Zebu' has permanent anchorage there. Riversway also hosts Preston's annual Maritime Festival.

Left: You might have heard of seeing double - but you ain't seen nothin' until you've viewed the delivery of 175 brand new panda cars accepted by the Lancashire Constabulary in 1967. The Lancs boys in blue were always at the forefront when it came to innovations - even experimental ones such as mobile policing - that helped them solve crime. The cars, pictured here at the constabulary's headquarters, were duly driven away to be put into service in every division in the county. When panda cars were first introduced they were the forerunners of a completely new type of task force. The experiment was proved to be a success, with a 10pc saving on manpower and a 20pc reduction in crime. Detection of crime increased from 27pc to 42pc. The cars kept in touch by means of personal radio; yet another first for the Lancashire force to chalk up.

The first cars had a livery of light blue with a white panda stripe, and a Police sign prominently displayed. A total of £100,000 was spent on the new panda cars. Each car travelled around a hundred miles every day, and cost five old pence a mile to run. Those were the days!

Above: Lightweight fibreglass was the basic material for the sleek Bond motors that rolled off the production line at the Bond Motor Works in Ribbleton Lane, Preston, in October 1965. Add a Triumph chassis and running gear, and there you had the typical Bond car. The Mini Bond had been the company's choice to mount on their tableau a few years earlier in 1952 when they took part in the Trades and Industries Procession in that year's Preston Guild Merchant.

The 1970s Bond Bug was a firm favourite; follow the little car down the road, and the one thing you couldn't miss was its prominent axle. With most cars you never get to see an axle let alone have to keep it spruced up. But wash your Bug and you had to wash the axle too, that is, if you didn't want to be thought of as a slob! Bond cars are still popular among enthusiasts around Britain, and the high performance six cylinder sports models head the lists in the popularity stakes.

Above: Throughout much of World War Two the aerodrome out at Warton was in use by the American Air Force as Base Air Depot No 2. The job of servicemen on the base was to work on new aircraft from the States and make necessary modifications to the planes.

Towards the end of the 1940s a party of aircraft designers from English Electric moved in to work on the prototype Canberra plane. The site was developed further after work began on the prototype for the Lightning aircraft. To cope with the growing number of test flights of the Lightning the runway was extended, a new control tower was added and high speed wind tunnels were built. This superb photograph was taken in 1959; from left to right the young aviators are Desmond de Villiers, Peter Hillwood, Jimmy Dell and Roland Beaumont. They were captured by the camera standing alongside a pre-production batch of three sleek Lightning aircraft.

The Preston Guild

Below: One of the church processions passes along Fishergate past the front of the old Theatre Royal, where 'Ivanhoe' was playing, during the 1952 Guild celebrations. It is getting on for two hundred years since the Theatre Royal, once described as 'The most historic place of amusement in Preston', was opened in 1802. The chairman at that time was Mr H Siddons, whose wife, the versatile actress Sarah Siddons, played an amazing total of six different parts over a short period of time. In 1833 Watkins Burroughs took over, redecorating the interior and repainting the scenery. Seats at that time cost one and sixpence in the pit, and if you weren't too fussy, sixpence in the gallery. If you were one of the swells a box would set you back two and sixpence.

From 1869 there were various developments; films were first shown there in 1911. An impressive Christie Unit Organ and orchestra were added that would rise from the sunken pit to stage level. The theatre's popularity waned, however, and the building was eventually demolished. The ABC Cinema opened on the site on 14th March 1959, but after fighting a losing battle with television was soon forced to close its doors.

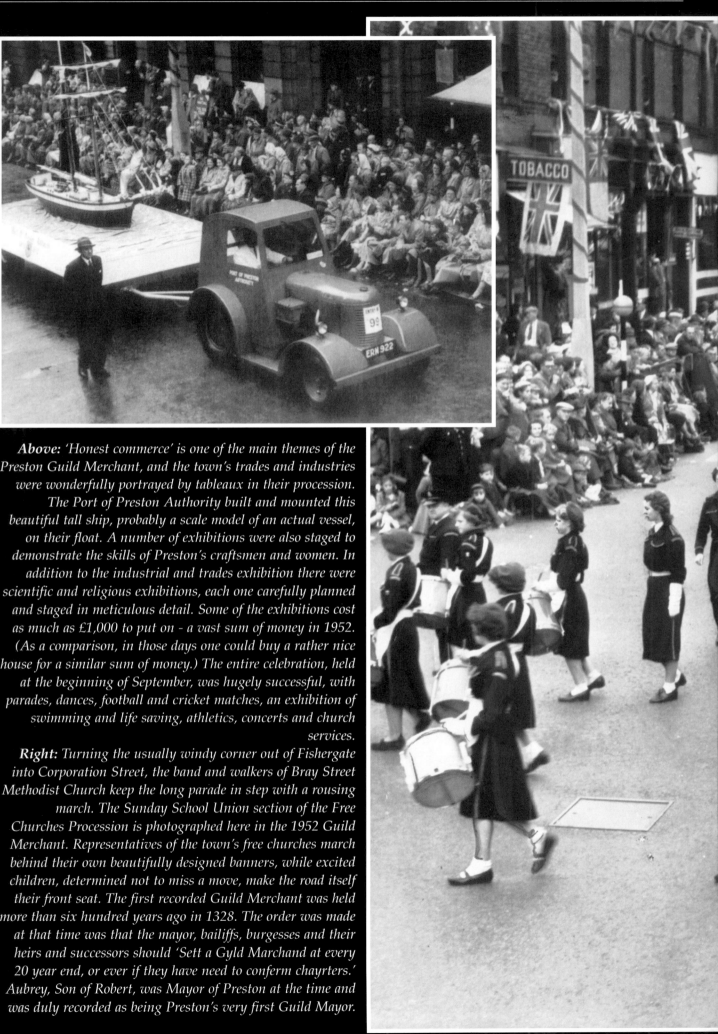

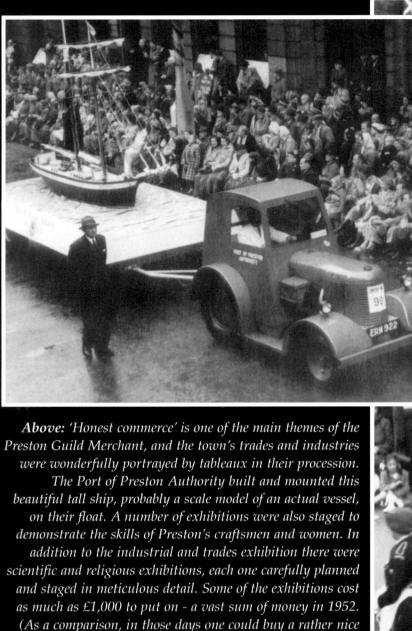

Above: 'Honest commerce' is one of the main themes of the Preston Guild Merchant, and the town's trades and industries were wonderfully portrayed by tableaux in their procession. The Port of Preston Authority built and mounted this beautiful tall ship, probably a scale model of an actual vessel, on their float. A number of exhibitions were also staged to demonstrate the skills of Preston's craftsmen and women. In addition to the industrial and trades exhibition there were scientific and religious exhibitions, each one carefully planned and staged in meticulous detail. Some of the exhibitions cost as much as £1,000 to put on - a vast sum of money in 1952. (As a comparison, in those days one could buy a rather nice house for a similar sum of money.) The entire celebration, held at the beginning of September, was hugely successful, with parades, dances, football and cricket matches, an exhibition of swimming and life saving, athletics, concerts and church services.

Right: Turning the usually windy corner out of Fishergate into Corporation Street, the band and walkers of Bray Street Methodist Church keep the long parade in step with a rousing march. The Sunday School Union section of the Free Churches Procession is photographed here in the 1952 Guild Merchant. Representatives of the town's free churches march behind their own beautifully designed banners, while excited children, determined not to miss a move, make the road itself their front seat. The first recorded Guild Merchant was held more than six hundred years ago in 1328. The order was made at that time was that the mayor, bailiffs, burgesses and their heirs and successors should 'Sett a Gyld Marchand at every 20 year end, or ever if they have need to conferm chayrters.' Aubrey, Son of Robert, was Mayor of Preston at the time and was duly recorded as being Preston's very first Guild Mayor.

Above: The 1952 Guild celebrations, and a group of young children with a charming Miss Muffet emphasise Safety First on the Hawkins Treasures tableau. The message appears to be targeting parents rather than the children themselves: 'Guard over your treasures' the message at the rear of the float tells us, while a sign beside Miss Muffet's seat urges parents to care for their young children. The children taking part here seem to be well enough cared for - they are having a whale of a time on what must have been a red letter day in their young lives. The Guild celebrations rounded off with a torchlight procession through the streets of Preston (what a wonderful sight that must have been!), and a huge firework display in Avenham Park gave the Guild Merchant a send off to remember - until the year 2012.

Facing page, top: This mammoth box of chocs was the ingenious work of Beech's Chocolates, who constructed this tasty tableau for the Preston Guild Merchant Procession. The two young workers in the tableau sit at a table, with weighing scales and sample boxes in front of them. Perhaps they threw handfuls of free sample goodies to the waiting crowd. The rest of the factory workers got to take part in the procession too; smart in their clean white overalls and neat caps, they walk behind their float.

The camera snapped Beech's tableau as it was passing the Old Black Bull. The date of this Guild Merchant was 1952, though in the normal run of things the event should have been staged in 1942. The first Guild Merchant was recorded in 1328, six years after Robert the Bruce pillaged and burnt the town of Preston, and though the event was a rather hit and miss affair in medieval times the Guild's 20 year interval had remained unbroken since 1542. The year that broke the mould was 1942; because the country was at war the Guild celebrations were postponed until 1952, making this particular festival the first for 30 years instead of the usual 20.

Strung out behind, the many other religious tableaux and church banners follow the walkers up Friargate towards the Market Square. A number of them, such as the young girl in the foreground of the photograph who represents an angel, are dressed appropriately for the procession. The history of Friargate itself goes back to beyond the 13th Century, and even in those far off days it was a well used thoroughfare. The road then led to a Franciscan friary that once stood on the site of Ladywell House in Marsh Lane. Even then the authorities had a problem with traffic; the narrow road was often blocked by members of the public who left such things as cart wheels in the road. A fine of ten shillings was levied on each item - an enormous amount of money in the 13th Century.

Above: In this photograph from the 1952 Guild celebration, devoted members of the congregation of the Sacred Heart Parish Church reverently carry Our Lady of Fatima in the Roman Catholic Procession. The base of the statue bears a prayer for penance.

Members of the cast of the 'Merrie England' show staged in Avenham Park wave enthusiastically to the crowds and the clicking cameras. These pretty girls in their colourful costumes (and what appears to be a solitary male on the right of the photograph) are having a wonderful time: those genuinely happy smiles the cast are wearing are obviously not put on for the occasion. Three performances of the Merrie England song and dance show were given in the park by the Preston Cecilian Choral Society and Preston Drama Club. The 1952 Guild Merchant celebrations featured every part of Preston life, and had church parades, dances, athletics, exhibitions, sporting events, a trades and industry procession and a vintage car rally. Preston and District Cricket League played Lancaster and District Cricket League in Moor Park, and for those who preferred soccer, Preston North End played the Swiss team Servett FC.

Below: The Bond Minicar - 'Made here in Proud Preston' - formed the tableau presented by the National Union of Vehicle Builders in the Trades Procession at the Preston Guild Merchant of 1952. 'MARK C' was the registration temporarily allotted to the car on this float, and we are left wondering what particular significance that had. At the time the Bond Mini Car claimed the title as the world's most economical car.

The procession, held on Wednesday 3rd September, started from Preston North End car park, travelled slowly along Deepdale Road and St George's Road, then through the town centre taking in Friargate, Fishergate and Church street before making its way back again to Deepdale Road.

All kinds of local trades were represented by tableaux in the parade: the town's textile industry had a 'Cotton through the Ages' float; the Port of Preston Authority mounted an elaborate ship, and the Ministry of Supply had an Atomic Energy tableau.

Right: The rather windswept girls on one of James Watt's tableaux are having a fantastic if rather chilly time as their vehicle passes the Old Black Bull public house (whose proprietor, by strange coincidence, was W.A. Watt. Were they related in any way, we wonder?). James Watt, whose premises were situated in Paley Road, were importers of timber, sawmillers and casemakers, and specialised in Neptune domestic woodwear. Their floats each carried examples of finished and partly finished joinery work. The Trades Procession at the Preston Guild Merchant of 1952 was held on Wednesday 3rd September, and the spectators along the route are obviously taking no chances with the vagaries of the British weather! Preston's many trades were proudly represented in the procession: brewers Matthew Brown & Co had a float; painters, bricklayers, stonemasons, plasterers, plumbers, all constructed their individual tableaux and played their part in the Guild celebrations.

The fashions worn by spectators in the crowd give us a clue to the fact that this parade is part of the 1972 Preston Guild Merchant. The limousines are part of the Church of England procession, and the banner being carried along in the background is that of St Oswald's Church.

Suede and leather was very much part of the 70s fashion scene, and in this short stretch of road you could buy the latest 'in' gear from two establishments. A shop on the left advertises 'Suede & Leather' while almost opposite is Suedewear. Nothing wrong with a little healthy competition.

Rainford's model shop, with its displays of racing cars, railway locomotives and track and plastic model kits, was a magnet for every young boy and perhaps their sisters as well.

The photograph is very atmospheric, like a moment frozen in time. Strange, isn't it, to think that the children watching this parade will be around thirty years old now, perhaps with families of their own, and the young couples who bought their trendy gear from Suedewear will now be pushing sixty. Gives you a creepy feeling, doesn't it?

Shopping Spree

Below: Doesn't this photograph make you want to pick up the little girl and her tricycle and place them safely on the pavement? But then, this was 1959, and though traffic levels in the town centre and on approach roads such as London Road were very high even at that time, estates such as Brookfield, where this picture was taken, would have been much less cluttered with cars. It is interesting to look back at the advertising on the day; it is just possible to make out the subject of some of the adverts outside J & J Dilworth's shop. The overt cigarette advertising is the first to catch the eye, and it comes as quite a shock to be told that Senior Service satisfy or Players please, or to be advised to smoke Old Holborn. The Vimto ad is much less controversial. It might surprise today's youngsters who still drink it to know that the fruit drink was around so long ago. But Vimto in fact goes back even further, at least to the 1940s (and possibly even earlier), when it was a favourite drink along with cream soda, sarsparilla and dandelion and burdock.

Right: Busy with cars as long ago as 1955, the traffic at this junction of Fishergate and Chapel Street is even more frenetic today. This view, looking in the direction of the Market Square, has changed somewhat, not least by the addition of a set of traffic lights which serves to keep vehicles on the move. Henry Dodgson were holding a sale at the time, and large windows full of bargains tempt people to invest in a new wardrobe. A rather nice class of clothing (note the Swears and Wells sign above the window) was sold at Henry Dodgson's store, and choice was across the board from dresses, coats and jackets to bridal wear - models in the front window display a bride's gown and bridesmaid's dress for sale. Dodgson's also advertised themselves as Furriers; this of course was many years before popular opinion began to turn against the wearing of fur. Back in the 1950s, fur, not to mention mink, was the badge of wealth and elegance worn by film stars and the upper classes.It was every woman's dream to own a luxurious coat of real fur. 'Fun' fur was to become popular twenty years on in the 1970s.

Above: The advertisements are without a doubt the most striking feature of this fascinating old photograph which dates back to the late 1940s or early 1950s. The wonderful McEwan's Export advert dominates the Gardner Street wall, and a bottle of McEwan's India Pale Ale is the subject of the ad. 'See what you get', the Meredith & Drew advert tells us alongside a picture of a cellophane wrapped packet of biscuits. Ready packed biscuits were catching on in the 1950s, but up to and well beyond this time grocers usually sold biscuits that were packed in tins with glass lids. The customer chose the biscuits and the grocer weighed them out from the tin. The see through packets advertised here were obviously a real innovation. Reginald Salberg's name was featured on the Royal Hippodrome's prominent advert. The theatre, situated in Friargate, was hosting the Preston Repertory Company's performance of 'Murder Mistaken' on Monday 7th September, and seat prices ranged from three and sixpence to a shilling. A real bargain.

Right: Remember Pegrams stores in Lune Street? In the 'good old days' before the mass 1960s takeover by self service supermarkets, the small grocer was an important part of every community. Even the signs on Peglers' windows, 'Groceries and Provisions' seem to say that this was one of the truly traditional grocers, the kind where you might have to wait in a queue, but when you reached the counter the personal service was worth waiting for. And if you were lucky you might even be lucky enough to find a chair or two to sit on while you waited.

Next door along is Singer's Army Stores, their specialist garments hanging outside to provide maximum temptation for passing punters to see and hopefully spend their money on. Almost the first thing we notice about the Army Stores is the absence of hands on the clock mounted on their building. What happened? Were the hands purposely removed for some reason, or did they simply drop off one day on to the head of some unlucky passer by? Makes your head ache to think of it....

Above: *The price was right and the food was finger lickin' good . . . did this elderly couple decide to take advantage of Kentucky Fried Chicken's trial offer of a whole chicken for eight shillings, or chicken and chips at two? Colonel Sanders and his famous recipe chicken was just about to make inroads into Britain - starting with Preston. Britain's very first Kentucky Fried Chicken establishment, opened in 1965, was rather unfortunately (for Wimpys at least) situated next to the already up and running and very popular Wimpy Bar, and though Prestonians loved a Wimpy they knew a bargain when they saw one. Wimpys was no doubt destined to go through a slack period until the novelty of KFC wore off. After all, they did charge one and sixpence for a chicken sandwich. But they also had buttered oatcakes, jam pasty and current squares on offer for a matter of a few coppers. Very tempting. On the other side of Kentucky Fried Chicken is Timothy White's Chemist. Long gone, of course, but remembered with affection. How the memories come flooding back!*

Left: *Older Prestonians will be sure to remember the strange feeling of walking for the first time around a self service store with a wire basket over their arm, choosing their own goods from the shelves. Many shoppers recall with nostalgia the days when they could ask their grocer for half a pound of bacon, a quarter of tea, two pounds of sugar (remember the blue bags?) and perhaps a couple of packets of crisps for the kids, always with a little blue bag of salt somewhere inside. The grocer would slice and weigh, cut and wrap, all the while chatting about the family, the war or the weather, with a personal service rarely seen in the impersonal supermarket of today. It really was like 'Open all Hours'! This most interesting photograph dates back to 1964 and was taken in one of Preston's very first self service stores, in Ribbleton Lane. The new method of shopping quickly caught on. Self service gave us the benefit of convenience. But did we at the same time lose some of the essence of our communities?*

Above: Captured in a few minutes of rare leisure time, these girls, who worked at Tulketh Spinning Co around 1922, look very cheerful in spite of the 48 hour week that mill workers were expected to work in those days. This was the normal state of affairs across the whole of the north of England, in the Lancashire cotton mills and in the woollen mills of Yorkshire. Starting time was typically 7am; at 8.30 there would be a half hour break for breakfast, after which they would work on from 9am till 12.30pm. After 45 minutes' lunch break they would carry on working until 5pm. Saturday morning was obligatory, and hours were usually from around 8am till 12 noon. A few older readers might just be able to remember their young days when they started work in the mill, learning weaving or spinning or some other job for half of each day while the rest of the day was spent in school. And all this at the tender age of twelve! Average pay for the youngsters was between four and sixpence and five shillings a week (around 25 pence).

Right: Women far outnumber the men in this 1919 photograph of a group of weavers at Centenary Mill in New Hall Lane, Preston. Young people as young as twelve often went into the mills while still attending school part time. As they grew older they would often work their way through a series of jobs within the mill, developing many skills in the textile industry and often staying in the same industry for the rest of their lives.

Weavers had more skills than weaving: learning to lip read was a must as when all the looms were running the noise in the room was deafening and people found it impossible to hear each other speak. In those long ago days - and for many years - mill workers everywhere faced danger on a day to day basis from the machinery they had to operate, some of which had to be cleaned while the machine was running. Every mill had its nasty accidents until legislation eventually brought in the safety standards we are accustomed to today.

From the war effort to the home front

No history of Preston would be complete without reference to the Royal Ordnance site at Chorley. Royal Ordnance can trace its roots back to the sixteenth century when the then Royal Ordnance Factories acquired land situated at Waltham Abbey. Land for today's factory at Chorley was purchased in 1937.

The early days

The construction of the 900 acre site contained within a perimeter fence over seven miles long, recorded some amazing statistics which bear testament to a community which played a crucial role in the war effort.

Over 15,000 people worked to complete the site just prior to the outbreak of World War II. The world's largest concrete mixer at 160 ft churned out 5,000 tons of concrete per day whilst construction was in progress.

When the site was completed, the renowned Lancashire songstress, Gracie Fields gave a special thank-you concert at Lisieux Hall to celebrate the tremendous efforts of the construction crews. The factory was officially opened in March 1939 by George VI and production began later that year.

Facing page: Foundations for one of the buildings - October 1939.
Above: A canteen under construction in 1937,
Below: A general view to the south of Shaw Brook dating from December 15th 1937.

The Second World War

During its heyday between the war years of 1939 and 1945 the factory, which became known as the Garden City, due to its greenery and well tended flower beds, employed over 30,000 staff operating a three shift system. Some employees travelled from as far afield as Fleetwood, making a journey of up to 25 miles by bus or rail. During the war years, munitions produced at the site ranged from small detonators to incredible 12,000 lb 'Tallboy' bombs.

After the war

After the war the company diversified and began breaking down ammunition, salvaging 250 tons of brass and steel per week.

The manufacture of prefabricated concrete 'Airey' houses was undertaken in the late 1940s, feeding the urgent need for housing in the post war years.

And today...

Today Royal Ordnance's main customer is the Ministry of Defence, procuring arms for the Navy, Army and Air Force. Internationally Royal Ordnance has customers in 60 countries competing in world wide markets such as Germany, France, South Africa, Israel and America.

Munitions produced by Chorley and Royal Ordnance are the benchmark against which others are measured.

Research plays a vital part of the work undertaken on the site with the Fast Event Facility, being unique in Europe, located in the heart of the complex. The facility has a dedicated high speed physics team able to record explosions and produce analytical breakdown of the 'fast' event, maintaining the site's unequalled world wide reputation in explosives technology.

Change
As we approach the millennium, the defence market is going through major change. A world wide reduction in defence spending has resulted in a shrinking market and Royal Ordnance, like others in the defence industry, has had to respond by restructuring its business.

Chorley site has undergone major changes since privatisation in 1985 and purchase by British Aerospace in 1987.

Above: Building work taking place in 1938.
Below: Automatic Shell Filling Plant in the late 1960s/early 1970s.

Since acquisition the number of employees has reduced to the small but efficient production site workforce of 120.

A new village

Exciting redevelopment opportunities are being progressed on the pats of the complex no longer used by Royal Ordnance.

The Company is working with Chorley, South Ribble and Lancashire County Council authorities to create a new village community.

Derelict industrial land is planned to be redeveloped to provide housing, offices, schools, leisure facilities, industrial units and warehousing facilities. The new community will have a reopened railway station, 1,500 new houses and as many as 10,000 new jobs could be created.

A sophisticated demolition and reclamation process will be carried out to remove all risk of contamination and leave clean, attractive, well serviced land for development.

Existing roads will be retained to serve the village, thus the pleasant countryside which became the factory complex in the thirties will once again play a constructive role in the future of the local community.

Above: A 105 mm Hesh Production Unit in the late 1970s.
Left: An aerial view of the Chorley site.

T Snape & Company - providing business with its printing needs for over a century

One of Preston's oldest-established businesses, T Snape & Company, printers, was founded by Thomas Snape round about 1858. From its premises in Boltons Court, the company supplied many of the town's local businesses, councils and health authorities with commercial print.

The first Annual Report of the Preston Royal Infirmary was printed by Snapes in 1870, the same year in which the company produced the annual report for the Blind Welfare Society. This society still remains one of the company's customers today.

As the business expanded, Thomas's son, Herbert Tracey Snape joined the company. On October 8th 1892 Thomas Snape arrived at work as usual. After talking for a while with his foreman, he went into his office. Five minutes later the same foreman found Thomas dead at his desk.

T. SNAPE & Co.,

COMMERCIAL

STATIONERS, PRINTERS,

AND

ACCOUNT BOOK MANUFACTURERS

141, CHURCH STREET;

Steam Printing Works :—11, BOLTON'S COURT.

PRESTON.

Sets of Account Books made to order on the shortest notice, in the most approved style, and at reasonable prices.

MILL STATIONERY OF EVERY DESCRIPTION.

Tracey Snape decided to take on John Sutton and Richard Shepherd as partners. Led by this triumvirate, the company became one of the first steam printers in the country and also the first to install Monotype keyboards and casters.

Many of the company's employees served with honour during the first war. The company survived this and continued trading through the depression of the twenties, becoming a limited company in 1927.

Tracey Snape died in 1935, aged 54. Richard Shepherd was left to run the company, making Sidney Barker company secretary and later a director of the company. During the thirties Richard's grandsons, Bernard Swarbrick and Dick Shepherd joined the company which continued to prosper. Richard died aged 79 in 1938 after a sixty year association with the company.

THE SIXTEENTH

ANNUAL REPORT

OF THE

PRESTON

Industrial Institute for the Blind,

For the Year ending March 31st, 1883.

Established in accordance with Resolutions passed at a Public Meeting held in the Town Hall, Tuesday, March 11th, 1867. The Mayor, EDMUND BIRLEY, Esq., in the chair.

Above: Notice displayed in shop window on 141 Church Street when first established.
Left: The 1883 Annual Report for the Blind Welfare.
Top left: Herbert Tracey Snape, son of Thomas Snape.

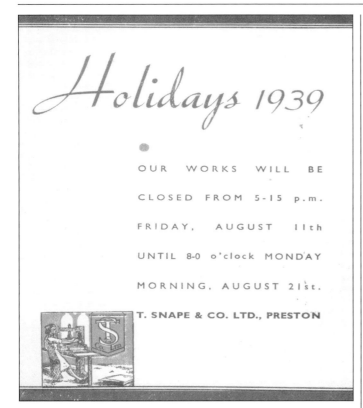

Holidays 1939

OUR WORKS WILL BE

CLOSED FROM 5-15 p.m.

FRIDAY, AUGUST 11th

UNTIL 8-0 o'clock MONDAY

MORNING, AUGUST 21st.

T. SNAPE & CO. LTD., PRESTON

When war was declared again in 1939, all the young men in the company were called up. During this difficult time Sidney Barker and his works manager Edward Howard kept the business going until Messrs Swarbrick and Shepherd returned from the war. The company was being managed at this time by the late Richard Shepherd's trustees with Sidney Barker as working director.

Just after the war, the company undertook one of its more unusual jobs. Sketches secretly drawn by Japanese prisoners of war relating to conditions in the camps were brought to Snapes. The small pieces of paper needed to be ironed out and line blocks made in order for the book to be printed. The book, entitled "In Defence of Singapore", was dedicated to the members of the North and East Lancashire Regiments who had been captured during the campaign.

Throughout the late forties and fifties the company grew and Snapes became well known for high quality goods and service. They were proud of the number of jobs they were given within Preston itself. For many decades, long runs of wine labels for a neighbouring and old established merchant were a regular task. In the parish church, only a few yards from the printing works itself, was-and is- a beautifully bound volume recording the names of 1,201 officers and men of the North Lancashire Loyal Regiment who died in the Second World War. Each name is printed in Monotype Dorchester script on goatskin parchment. The run was two! the job was produced in its entirety by Snapes.

Above: A leaflet announcing the company's holiday arrangements for 1939.
Below: One of the post war Wayzgoose.

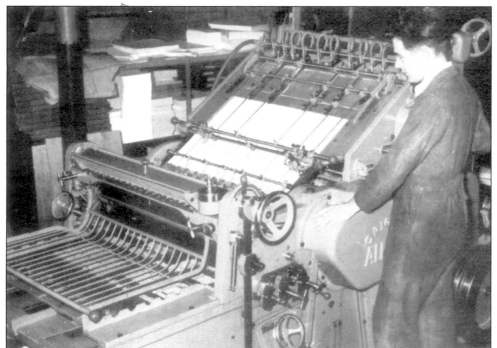

time consuming. A booklet of hints to authors that Snapes printed warned them to edit their copy carefully before submitting it for printing because alterations meant laborious and costly work. "Every single letter and punctuation mark is represented by a tiny piece of metal.

The printer has had to arrange these.... He locks the type in a steel frame to make what he calls a 'forme'. It takes great care and skill to do properly. But it must all be undone again before the smallest alteration can be made."

Every year, the company took its employees on a day trip, known as a Wayzgoose. Blackpool and the Lakes were among the favourite and most visited places and these days out were much appreciated by the workforce.

On the death of Sidney Barker, Dick Shepherd and Bernard Swarbrick became joint managing directors of the company, with responsibility for its day to day running. Michael Prior was appointed company secretary. The company's name was by now well known throughout the UK and abroad.

In July 1976, Dominic Swarbrick, son of Bernard and great grandson of Richard Shepherd, joined the company which continued, with mixed fortunes to the end of the decade with Frank Ryan as works manager.

The company continued to flourish through investment, the first offset litho being purchased in the early sixties. Work on the old machines was becoming too

Top: A new letter press machine installed - early 1950s.
Above: A woodcut of the building, still recognisable today.
Right: (left to right) Steve, Mick, Gavin and Dave with new C.P. Tronic Press installed in 1998.

His place was taken by Adrian Corcoran who had joined the firm in 1979.

The technological changes within the printing industry was gathering pace, so that yet more new equipment was needed at Snapes. Two Heidelberg presses were bought and Apple Mackintosh computers replace the now-outdated compugraphic equipment. New folding and collating machines were installed and 1998 saw the company purchase its first CP Tronic two-colour Heidelberg press.

By 1982, when Dominic Swarbrick was made a director, the printing industry was going through great changes. New investment was needed to keep the company ahead of its rivals. After over a hundred years using letterpress, a complete change to litho had to be made. During this year the company installed computerised typesetting. New offset presses were bought, together with modern finishing equipment.

Over the next ten years there were changes in management. First Dick Shepherd retired in 1985 after over fifty years with the company. Sadly he lived to enjoy only four years of retirement. In the nineties, ill health caused the works manager, Frank Ryan to retire after more than forty years service.

Bernard Swarbrick, now in his sixtieth year with the company, is The Chairman and retains a keen interest in its affairs and the continuing modernisation of the Company's plant and equipment. , His son Dominic has taken over as Managing Director.

The firm's reputation for high quality print at the right price, delivered on time, was first earned by Thomas Snape and has remained intact ever since. The company still supplies many businesses in and around Preston with colour brochures, stationery, leaflets, folders and books. Everything is produced under one roof. The firm prides itself on the loyalty of its staff and owes much of its success to the people who have worked there over the years.

The company has seen many changes since its foundation, has survived two world wars and numerous recessions and has taken part in seven Preston Guilds. Hopefully, it will see another hundred years - not the biggest printer in the area but one that prides itself on high quality work from a loyal staff.

Above: Dominic in front of the company van 1997.
Left: Grandsons of the late Richard Shepherd, Dick ((left) and Bernard (right).

Chris Miller - moving memories

The original founder of Chris Millers came to Preston from Westmoreland in 1837 with a horse and cart and very little else.

For many years his operations were small and localised, but when his grandson, the late Mr Chris Miller, took over the firm at the beginning of the century -with little capital and equipment- there came the beginning of its modern progress.

He expanded his firm into the specialised job of timber hauling which required hard work and initiative. He continued his general haulage alongside the new specialisation.

For many years horses did all the pulling and carrying. The company bought its first petrol lorries in 1921 and all horse transport was eventually disposed of in 1935. By 1960 the sons of Chris, Jack and Arthur, had a fleet of 30 vehicles, 25 trailers and seven mobile cranes at the Miller headquarters in Croft Street, Preston. The work they did was divided into general haulage and 'special' haulage which involved particularly heavy or awkward loads. Haulage in a port like Preston involves many different commodities including raw materials for mills, finished textiles for export, newsprint, oil, beer and groceries amongst them. The 'awkward' type of load included plant and machinery, long girders and boats. , The development of mobile cranes in the 1960s and 70s further enhanced the company's abilities, with its growing fleet regularly utilised in all manner of lifts around the area.

These assorted techniques allowed Millers to continue to expand their operations. A change in the family involvement occurred when the fifth generation took

Millers, used their experience and their big Mack, 'Bonzo Bear'. It was the latter vehicle that was featured in the press but Millers' tubs and girders that did the bulk of the work.

The recession of the early eighties was to have an effect. When Joshua Tetley re-organised under their new owners Ind Coope, who had their own fleet, Millers lost contract work for ten vehicles. Other work too dried up and the port of Preston was closed resulting in a big reduction in work for the company and its 40,000 square feet of warehousing.

over in the late sixties. It consisted of the third Chris Miller and his cousin John. Over the years they have been involved in some strange jobs. One of the most memorable was delivering rock used in the construction of the Seaforth Container terminal. Several firms tried to do the job. All gave up due to wear and tear caused by the heavy loads and rough ground at Seaforth. Millers agreed to a one week trial. Their solution used regular vehicles from the quarry at Seaforth, then, more expendable equipment for the final haul across the construction site. The trial period became a full year's work and over 120,000 tons of rock were moved.

At the end of the seventies Millers made the headlines again with another huge job successfully completed. This one was moving all the water-handling equipment for Dinorwic Power Station. Originally planned as 24 voyages of an expensive ro-ro heavy lift vessel, the job was trimmed to just seven when

However the space was soon put to good use, producing aluminium roofing sheets for a German company. The sheet was part of a 'state-of-the-art' system which allowed architects to design large span roofs without joints or fixing holes. The result was some very long sheets - up to 140' (43.2m). These were manufactured in Croft Street and delivered on the company vehicles throughout Britain.

Above: Two trusty Atkinsons with their Gardner engines. Top: A "Speed Crane" at the rear with an AEC Mercury being loaded with lathes. Left: The heavy gang with their tackle vans, forklift and crane in the yard, circa 1968. Facing page, top: A trolley bus built by Dick Kerr being transported to Yorkshire. Facing page, bottom: The petrol engined Leyland fleet with Chris Miller and his sons, Jack and Arthur, outside the company premises, circa 1922.

During the early 1990s the business continued with its various lifting, transport and handling activities both locally and more nationally. The knack which the Miller men had inherited and developed was still very much in demand. The need to lift and shift heavy or awkward loads remains - and to date there is no computer available to perform this work. The old Prestonian saying 'You'll need Chris Millers to move that' remains as true today as over the decades.

In 1987 the company quietly celebrated its 150th birthday. At the time Chris Miller attributed the successful years to the company being "small, resourceful and reliable". At this stage the fleet had kept pace with the changing times and included a modern fleet of telescopic cranes, forklifts, vehicles and specialist trailers, all operated by a team of first class experienced personnel.

Corgi have recently included a set of model vehicles from the Miller fleet in their 'Classic' range of heavy haulage vehicles. There are other reminders of the company's work around Preston; for example the E. H. Booth Clock Bridge, the two Nelson Buoys at the entrance to Riversway and the stone sculptures outside the Corn Exchange were all positioned by the company with care and a pride in the town.

Above left: The Corgi models. **Top:** A 150 ton valve passes through Huddersfield with pulling and pushing tractors en route to Dinorwic Power Station. **Left:** 'Bonzo Bear' hauls a storage tank though Blackpool to I.C.I. Hillhouse.

Attwater & Sons Ltd - progress through innovation

The products made by the family firm of Attwater & Sons Ltd can be found inside planes and even old trams, but they are seldom seen.

Richard Attwater did not know when he started up in business that he was founding a little industrial dynasty, but 130 years and four generation on his business is still within the family and every generation has given the firm a boss called Richard.

Mill. It advertised "Steam Engine and Hydraulic Packings' which included fire brigade hose and appliances, chemical fire "extincteurs", Dobbie and Jacquard furnishings, linen thread, cards and mails.

Under the heading 'Electrical Engineers' Sundries' it was selling Canadian and Indian amber mica, dynamo tapes, hollow braids, Empire cloths,

This company, one of Preston's oldest firms, began in Bluebell Yard, Church Street. It was founded to produce plaited steam packings for the town's mills and offer chandlery services for the tall ships and steam ships at Preston docks.

An advertising leaflet for 1897 features an amusing trade mark in which a cockerel, minus its crest perches on one leg on top of a globe. A flier over it announces, "While I live, I'll crow." Attwaters' Combination, pure asbestos and flax with anti-friction lubricant is offered at 1s 2d per lb. Pure asbestos yarn is 1s 5d and dagger packing, whatever that may be, is 2s 7d.

By the time the Preston Guild Souvenir Handbook for 1902 came out the company was based at 109, Church Street and Hopwood Street

Above: Richard Henry Attwater.
Above right: An early brochure cover.
Right: The firm's original premises with Richard Attwater, founder of the company, standing proudly at the door.

ebonite and Vulcanized fibre sheet rod and tubes, asbestos ribbons, paper, sheets and all insulating materials. Its registered trade mark featured a bowls player with a medal round his neck and the company telephone was National 45!

Above: Ramsey MacDonald viewed an eclipse of the sun through Mica Spectacles, manufactured by Attwater & Sons, from special Amber Mica mined by them at their Finmarken Mines.
Below: An early workshop photograph at Hopwood Street.

The Prime Minister, Ramsay MacDonald viewed an eclipse of the sun through Mica spectacles manufactured by Attwaters from special Amber Mica mined by the company at their Finmarken Mines. On another occasion, round about the same time, the Lord Mayor of Manchester and a party of 70 councillors took a trip into the Mardale Tunnel of the Manchester Corporation Waterworks clad in waterproof garments supplied by the company.

Attwaters also supplied the hundreds of pairs of rubber thigh boots, rubber sheeting and hosepipes to the contractors, the Francois Cementation Company Ltd.

In 1913 the company found a commercially acceptable way of producing laminated plastic and has been doing this one way or another ever since. By 1919 the company was announcing itself "Contractors to War Office & Admiralties, British, American, Russian, Italian and French Governments."

It came to its present Hopwood Street works in 1904 but has also at different times been at Singleton Row (Lancaster Row), Gaskell Road (Penwortham), and a big old cotton mill in Pole Street. The present managing director, Richard Attwater came new to the business13 years ago. Previously he had been Trident submarine designer at Vickers' Barrow shipyard, having always been an electrical engineer, so that he was well prepared to lead the family business.

He has admitted that his is not the most glamorous of businesses but he points out that, over the years, Attwaters have been turning out the essentials of industry that other firms across the world relay on. Such is the constancy of their work that they are still producing some of the same lines begun in the twenties, and a few from even earlier.

However the firm is also forward-looking and the start of the nineties saw no less than ten new products in the Hopwood Street pipeline. Attwater insulation can be found in Royal Navy ships and RAF jets as well as trains across the world and trams on the front at Blackpool.

Attwaters are constantly forging new links with industries and businesses world wide. Since overseas clients are often entertained at the Preston factory the company has recently installed smart new office facilities, a new machine shop with new computer-controlled machinery. The order book is full and several new projects are under development. The continued success of this pioneering and innovative company seems well set to flourish for another 130 years.

Above: 70 councillors took a trip into the Mardale Tunnel of the Manchester Corporation Waterworks clad in waterproof garments supplied by the company.

Craftsmen bakers buying together and growing together

It was in the early sixties that several independent Craftsmen bakers decided to form a regional buying co-operative to be called North Western Bakers. Its purpose would be to provide other bakers in their area with a whole range of high quality ingredients more competitively priced through bulk buying.

When regional buying had proved a success, it was expanded on a national scale to form Bako UK. Five managers, one representing each region's co-operative, would meet monthly to decide which commodities should be purchased at what price and from whom, so that all member bakers would benefit from the spending power of a national organisation.

In order to identify more closely with the scheme, North Western Bakers' directors (all practicing craftsmen bakers) decided to change its name to Bako North Western, utilising Bako's contacts with world leading suppliers. Bako North Western's members can be economically supplied with a wide range of over 2,000 bakery raw materials in ambient, frozen and chilled form. These range from traditional staple goods such as fats, sugar and chocolate to high quality finished goods.

Handling and delivering the goods is efficient and prompt, organised by Bako's computerised warehouse management system. Appropriate, multi-temperature wagons transport goods to customers in prime condition. A large percentage of Bako North Western's fleet comprises 26-tonne multi-temperature delivery vehicles supplied by Gray & Adams of Doncaster, an acknowledged leader in the design and construction of this type of vehicle.

Bako North Western have recently moved into draw bar distribution systems suitable for delivering ambient chilled and frozen goods to customers located at the extremes of their distribution area. The current chilled range includes over 50 different sandwich fillings. Orders for these are taken by sales staff up to midday. They are produced in the evening and delivered to Bako in Preston before midnight for immediate onward despatch.

The co-operative began life in Warrington 26 years ago as a small office. The first storage facility was a tiny warehouse in New Hall Lane, Preston. A move came just two years later to a converted mill in Ribbleton Lane, Preston. However, the building's age and condition meant that the company spent a lot of time and money on maintenance, hence the management looked for a more permanent home. Other locations were considered however Preston was equidistant from the majority of the company's customers and the motorway system was excellent.

The company, on the advice of the Central Lancashire Development Corporation,

purchased. This now supports the project currently being undertaken to double the size of the warehousing facility with new goods inwards facilities, a test bakery and additional office capacity.

The remaining expansion land will be developed in phases as it is needed, says Managing Director Alan Williams, 'Bako North Western is here for the long run. So, rather than take a short term view, we decided to purchase sufficient land to accommodate our building plans for the forseeable future.'

Bako North Western now boasts a workforce of eighty employees and an annual turnover of £25 million. The company also has strong links with Bako Europa, a network of bakers co-operatives throughout Europe and Scandinavia.

The company's commitment to quality and high service levels is reflected by its continuous staff development programme, as evidenced by ISO 9002 and Investors in People accreditation.

decided to look at building opportunities on Roman Way Industrial Estate and subsequently built 20,000 sq. ft. of warehousing loading bays and offices.

Within five years the company had added a further 10,000 square feet of warehousing.

Two years later, additional office accommodation was erected together with a six-hundred pallet chilled and frozen storage facility.

In the interim, further expansion land had been

Above: A lorry making a delivery in the late 1980s.
Above left: The premises from above.
Facing page, top: A brochure dating from the 1970s.
Facing page, bottom: An company exhibition in the early 1970s.
Below: The new style lorries.

Lighting up lives all across the north

In 1887, at 89 Fishergate, Preston, Mr Edward Dewhurst founded his telephone engineering business. He was well qualified to do so, having served an apprenticeship with Mather & Platt in Manchester and worked for them for some time.

The business in Fishergate grew and developed over the following six years. Mr Edward Dewhurst's elder son, also Edward, took charge of the retail outlet. Miss Constance Dewhurst became managing director and chairman. The auto-electrical side of the business was managed

by Mr Arnold Dewhurst and Miss Caroline Dewhurst served as company secretary. In the beginning, equipment consisted of wooden trunking and the switchgear they made was mounted on slate! After six years a move was made to Mount Street. An advertisement from an 1896 edition of St Walburge's Schools' Gazette gives us a picture of what the firm's men were busy

with. It offers customers estimates for the lighting of shops, offices and private residences by electricity which is obviously quite an innovation. Also available was 'a large assortment of Incandescent Lamps and Shades. During the wars the company was required for munitions work, the electrical staff wiring aircraft hangars.

Today, the company's main markets are local authorities, commercial and industrial companies, the aerospace industry and the Water and Health Authorities. Also, control equipment is sold abroad, particularly to the Middle and Far East. The chief products are trunking, cable trays, conduits, lighting, fire alarms and closed-circuit television. Airfield lighting control systems are made in conjunction with British Aerospace. Systems have been supplied for Warton, for Howarden near Chester and for Birmingham International Airport.

The company has been awarded ISO 9001 certification and prides itself on its service to industry and the quality of its workmanship. The management is always looking for advances in technology and have recently begun to work with special, high-voltage equipment. Plans for the future include the supplying of airfield lighting in general and emergency lighting systems and standby lighting for runways.

The family connection has remained strong. Edward Dewhurst, the founder's grandson is now Managing Director and his sons, John and Paul are also Directors.

Above: Mr. Edward Dewhurst, founder of the company. Left: The firm's original premises at 89, Fishergate, from which it traded for six years.

The builder who was too small

Marl is the name given to a good type of soil, a mixture of clay, sand and lime, and this is probably the origin of the family name. These also happen to be the basic constituents of bricks and so building is probably in the Marland blood.

The story goes that Marland Brothers Limited was founded because Mary Emma Marland was so incensed when one of her sons was paid less than the going rate by a building contractor because he was considered to be too short to do a good job.

Whatever the truth of this, the company was started in 1907 with money belonging to Mrs Marland. The first builders were her sons Roland and George. Another son, Samuel was the book-keeper who became the first chairman when the company went limited in 1937, with brothers Caleb, Thomas and Henry and sister, Hannah who were the first shareholders.

The parcel of land from the north side of Liege Road and from the east side of Eden Street in Leyland was Marland property bought from a James Brown of Eden Street. Roland also bought a field in 1930 from Ezra Clarkson for £115. It now accommodates four bungalows, a terrace of four houses and the converted bungalow which is used as the Marland brothers' office.

The first phase of building was in Liege Road, providing bungalows for the family and management. They used the latest techniques and

At this time transport was by handcart. There was a mortar mixer in the yard and concrete was mixed by hand. Nowadays, of course, the firm has its full complement of JCBs, wagons and concrete mixers.

had solid composition floors with terrazzo tiles laid in the entrance halls. No electricity was laid on, the properties relying on gas for heating, cooking and lighting. A wash house with gas boiler was attached at the rear. These bungalows were completed in 1925.

In 1940 the brothers kept the office work at 21 Eden Street where the front rooms were fully equipped for business and Samuel Marland lived in the back with sister Prudence next door.

It was the early sixties before new offices were taken and now the company management is in its fourth generation of Marlands. The name is well known locally and plenty of work flows in from housing associations, local authorities and private development.

Above: Roland Marland. *Left:* St. Andrew's Vicarage, Leyland. *Top left:* Samuel Marland. *Facing page, top left:* George Marland. *Facing page, top right:* Mary Emma Marland. *Facing page, bottom:* The workforce in 1932.

James Mercer (Preston) Ltd - providing ideal conditions for over sixty years

James Mercer (Preston) Limited was formed by James (Jim) Mercer in 1936. He established his company in premises known as the Canal Bridge Works which were on the corner of Greenbank Street and Victoria Street. Using experience gained whilst working as a foreman heating engineer at Dilworth & Carr Limited, he offered heating and ventilation services.

Using solid fuel boilers and cast iron pipework with caulked joints, his men carried equipment to local jobs on handcarts when this was possible. If not transport was by bus or rail. If the job undertaken was more than a few miles away the men lived in lodgings, returning home only every two weeks.

The company was incorporated in 1941 and Jim's son, also called Jim, joined his father in the business. Sadly, Jim Mercer junior died during his father's working lifetime and so Tom Moxham was invited to become a company director, joined in 1955 by Dick Hayes and Jim Curran. Tom Moxham and Jim Curran died prematurely in 1963 and 1966 respectively.

When it became obvious that an office was needed in a locality before work could be obtained, it was decided to open one in Ormskirk in 1957. Another change became necessary the following year. Due to the compulsory purchase of the premises at Canal Bridge Works, alternative premises were needed and the company bought Tulketh Hall Works.

The ownership of the company was retained by the Moxham and Curran families and its management was administered by Dick Hayes. He was assisted by Brian Court and Harry Hornby who later became directors. The next generation, in the persons of John Moxham and Bill Curran, joined the company from school in 1965 and 1964 respectively and in their turn became directors. John Moxham was appointed managing director in 1982 and retains that position presently.

The company has always carried out work for local authorities and health authorities and enjoys a good reputation for completing satisfactorily all the work it undertakes. Turnover in 1941 was £4,800. Ten years later it had reached £21,000 and twenty years after that £910,000. The current turnover is in the region of £7 million. Mercers have carried out the installation of heating and hot and cold water services in and around Preston for such organisations as the Guild Hall, British Aerospace at Warton and Samlesbury, the Royal Preston and Sharoe Green Hospitals and the University of Central Lancashire.

A Service and Maintenance Operation was set up in 1991 which now has 10 service engineers. Expansion made it necessary to have more office accommodation and extra property was bought adjacent to the existing premises in Hesketh Street in 1994. The company has facilities for off site prefabrication of pipework, the manufacture and installation of ventilation ductwork and is able to carry out contracts to the value of over £1 million.

The current number of employees is 115. The company runs 32 small vans to transport men to sites, together with a 3 ton truck for deliveries.

Above: James Mercer provided the installations for the Preston Guild Hall. Left: One of the first Mini vans in Preston. Facing page, top: Heating, ventilation and water supplied the Preston Magistrates Courts.

EH Booth & Co - traditionally better

The firm of E H Booth & Co Ltd was founded by Edwin Henry Booth, a man of outstanding character and ability. He was very proud of the business he had set up declaring that he sold the best goods he could buy, in shops staffed with first class assistants and that customers should not expect him to run after them.

He imported special French wines and brandies and chartered a ship to bring in a cargo of tea and other groceries for the opening of Preston Dock. When the first Electric Supply Company in Preston nearly failed he went to its rescue as he had faith in the future of electricity.

When he died in 1899 he was one of the best-known men in the district round Preston. His early hardships had made him sympathetic to the poor and all in trouble. He had co-founded an orphanage, been treasurer for the Homes for the Blind and on the committee of the Royal Cross Trust for the deaf and dumb. While he lived, no good cause in Preston was left unanswered.

It is now 150 years since Mr Booth opened his first small shop in Blackpool. He put his four sons in turn into the business but Edwin left to take up the wholesale tea trade in London and Fred became a doctor, serving as Medical Officer of Health for St Anne's on sea. The eldest, John, however, was of great help to him, becoming in 1881 a junior partner with his father and gradually taking over responsibility until, on the death of Mr Booth senior in 1899 he became chairman of the company.

E. H. BOOTH & Co.,
TEA MERCHANTS,
WINE IMPORTERS,
Family Grocers, &c.,
PRESTON : 4, FISHERGATE ;
Blackpool : Market Street ;
CHORLEY : 38 & 39, MARKET St.;
LYTHAM : PARK STREET ;
Wholesale Department :
9, GLOVER'S COURT.
PRESTON.

Families may rely upon obtaining the best articles, on the most reasonable terms, at the above Establishments.

All Goods delivered by our own vans. 2½ per cent. discount on all orders of 20/- and upwards if paid for when ordered.

Above: The first account book of EH Booth.
Left: Preston Market Place in 1844.
Centre left: An early brochure cover.
Top left: Edwin Henry Booth, who founded the empire.

Customers came in their carriages and the good housewife took a great interest in the quality and prices of goods. Long credit was taken, bills paid yearly or half yearly and it needed a stout-hearted grocer to stand out for his due.

Mr John had been delicate as a boy and was sent on a voyage to the Mediterranean. Visiting Greece and Turkey gave him a special interest in cargoes of currants and sultanas from ports he had visited.

The business had been made a private limited company three years before. John Booth's co directors were his youngest brother Tim and a faithful employee, William Tattersall.

In these early days sugar was bought in great casks and was generally dark in colour. Lump sugar came in tall white cones and there was a chopping machine for it, worked by a foot pedal. Soft soap came in kegs and a trick played on new boys was to tell them to put their fingers in and have a good taste!

Above: A Group photograph taken outside Barton Hall. Mr John Booth, who took over from his father can be seen seated in the middle. Right: Chorley shop front in the 1930s.

On the occasion of his Golden Wedding all 349 members of staff wrote congratulations to John and his wife Ada. Their early married life was spent at St Anne's but he had moved to Preston to be nearer his father. The couple lived at Barton Hall where the staff were entertained on 'bonus day'. John Booth had begun a profit sharing scheme for the staff in 1909.

About 1900 a gown shop in Blackburn was bought and turned into another Booth store. It was decided to make the large upstairs rooms into the company's first cafe. People in those days did not have the cafe habit but still the venture prospered. Later, property in Fishergate was bought, with further adjoining houses alongside gradually being added. Both Mr Wyn and Mr Kenny, his sons, served in the armed forces during the First World War.

When it was over Booths began acquiring local shops, the first two at Ashton and Leyland.

Mr John died in 1941 by which time his two elder sons, Mr Wyn and Mr Kenny were well established in the business. They had been given responsibility from an early age and in due time became directors, meanwhile training up two of the fourth generation of Booths to join the family business.

Following the company centenary in 1947 it continued to trade successfully in the traditional pattern. Mr Wyn died in 1951 and Mr Kenny succeeded him as chairman. By the mid fifties sales had reached £1 million, a notable figure for those days.

Above: Mr John Booth. Top: Booths shop and café, Fishergate, Preston in the 1930s. Left: John Booth addressing staff on Bonus Day in the 1930s.

North Shore, Blackpool in the 1930s.

From the end of the second war until 1960, every year was a record year. Then came the challenge of the supermarket. Sales stopped increasing and since one third of business was on credit it was not possible to cut prices, though, of course, wages had to rise. 1961 saw a 2% loss of trade. If Booths were to have a future it would have to be on a new basis. Fulwood and Leyland were chosen as the company's first self service stores. Customers declared, "You won't see me with a wire basket", and "You're making a dreadful mistake, Mr Booth", but in 1962 sales increases of 3 1/2% were announced. By 1963 Preston, the firm's most profitable store had been successfully converted.

The sixties were a story of ever-increasing success. All Booths new business was in cash, so they moved to phase out the order trade by putting on a delivery charge and gradually increasing it. Delivery vans were gradually disposed of and credit eliminated. These new policies brought sales to £2 million by 1966.

Since resources were being used for conversion there were no new shops for a while.

Ashton was unsuitable for conversion and was closed. To compensate a new store was opened in Woodplumpton Road.

Sadly, Mr Kenny died, aged 78, in July 1970. He had been with the company for 60 years. Mr John succeeded as chairman and work continued. The shop at Longton was rebuilt and extended in 1971.

In September 1973 Edwin J Booth joined the firm, representing the fifth generation of the family.

On the staff side, more attention was paid to the recruitment of well educated boys under a trainer-manager scheme, so that the teams running the improved stores were second to none. Fresh meat became available in all stores, its ordering overseen by fresh meat controller Mr Smith who provided new skills to Booths' considerable previous experience.

1975 saw the opening of the Garstang store. Later in the same year a very good purchase was made. Looking for a replacement for the small though prosperous Fulwood store, Booths discovered that the asking price for the plot they wanted at Sharoe Green was £250,000. However, the vendor came under financial pressure and in 1974 agreed to accept £42,000 provided the money was immediately available. It became the very first 'Booths' Shopping Centre' which set the style for future development. It opened in 1978.

In 1975 Mr Simon Booth joined the firm, becoming a director in 1984. Already the Sharoe Green site had become too small for the very profitable trade there. The sales floor was enlarged and the fruit and vegetable area was much improved. Sharoe Green had become the leading store in both sales and profits.

At this time it was decided to close the last of the Booths' cafes, that at Preston. With the decline of Afternoon and 'high' tea, the style had become outdated.

1986 was a record year with profits of £1,352,000. In 1987 Mr Graham Booth joined the Board alongside his brother. In the following year the Preston store was closed. It had been losing business because of its lack of a car park. Waterstones, the booksellers, took over the shop but the head office remained in Glover's Court.

The experiment of 1997 was to build the first store in Yorkshire, at Ilkley, and the company feels confident that it is able to please the increasing number of people who look on it as 'traditionally better'.

Left: This picture, dating from 1965 shows the construction of the new Booths store in Chorley.
Facing page, top left: A vintage delivery van outside the company's Ribbleton store.
Below: Booths at Sharoe Green Lane, Fulwood. Preston in 1978.

PH Chandler (Leyland) Ltd - quality furniture for over forty years

In 1950 Mr Peter Henderson Chandler set himself up in business making the frames for three piece suites and fireside chairs.

His previous experience included being a chef in the army and a furniture maker in Edinburgh. Since his wife, Mrs Elsie Chandler and Mrs Vera Stringfellow, his sister in law also worked in the business, maybe his army cooking skills came in useful when they were busy with customers or office work!

In 1950 the premises, which were all purchased for £1000, were just one shed, measuring 1,800 square feet on the site in Talbot Road, Leyland which is still the company headquarters. He was equipped with a circular saw and a band saw, drills, planing machines and a spindle machine and the material he worked on was home-grown beech.

Left: Mr P. H. Chandler. Above: Mrs Elsie Chandler. Below: The original workshop.

His wife's father obliged with an interest-free loan. At the end of the first year his property and assets were valued at £3,090 15s 8d and cash at the bank amounted to just £31 0s 8d. There were more expenses than the man in the street might realise. Materials and carriage had cost £1,893 3s 4d and wages just £696 15s 9d. Other expenses had included lighting, rates, the running expenses of a motor van,

repairs and resharpening saws, insurance, accountancy, bank charges, stationery and office sundries.

Above: Mr P. W. Chandler as an apprentice in his father's car.
Right: An aerial shot of the site.

His profit for the year was £419 5s 5d, not unsatisfactory at fifties' values.

The business has shown a steady increase in size and profitability over the years. When larger premises were needed there was space to build on to the existing structures. There have been hiccups in the form of fires and bad debts but there has been little to hold up the transition from a modest beginning to the firm's becoming one of the UK's major contract furniture manufacturer.

Nowadays the beech used in the factory is imported and partly machined. Equipment includes a CNC router, multidrills, sanding machines and an automatic paint line.

Three generations of Chandlers have taken their parts in the business. Mr Peter H Chandler is currently the chairman at 83 years old, his son, also Peter, is managing director and Mrs Carol Chandler is a company secretary. Steven Chandler, Sharon Fisher and Julie Chandler are also directors.

The firm produces over 100,000 units a year which include tables, tops, chairs, stools, settles and rockers. If something a customer requires is not in stock it can be specially made by some of the 55 strong staff in the 40,000 square feet factory. Some of the company's specialities are bar, club-restaurant, hotel furniture and good quality domestic furniture, and luxury leather upholstery. There is no minimum order requirement and single items are given the same care as furniture for whole organisations. Deliveries are made nationwide.

Above: A vintage delivery van.

"THE FIRM PRODUCES OVER 100,000 UNITS A YEAR, INCLUDING TABLES, CHAIRS AND ROCKERS"

Proud of its past - confident of its future

In 1909 the founder of the business, Richard Bamber used a horse and cart to collect and deliver the second hand furniture he bought and sold. He took the premises in the old Sir Simon, now the Bello Restaurant and lived on the premises.

Bambers has always been very much a family business. The founder's son Harry and daughter

Jessie joined their father, helped by Jessie's husband for a short while. Now Harry's sons, Richard and Donald are the next generation of management assisted by their wives, Jean and Dorothy. Their sister, Helen, was also very much part of the business until her marriage to John Dick, a dealer in antiques, and her consequent move to Scotland.

They now run a successful furniture business near Glasgow with their son, Bruce.

The younger generation in Bambers are Richard's daughter Sarah and husband David and Donald's daughters, Gillian and Susan.

The present shop in Friargate is just across the road from the original one. It has gradually increased in size as more property has been purchased. Originally the tripe shop and ladies hat shop were bought together with the stables, then the mill at the back and a do-it-yourself shop to increase the frontage, finally three terraced houses to give better access to the road.

They have exported furniture to Europe and the USA They stock a wide variety in their 12,000 sq ft of showroom, and the staff endeavour to suit the tastes of each individual customer, whether they are in their teens or their nineties or somewhere in between.

Above: Harry Bamber receiving the award for Best Stand in the Trades Show at the Public Hall in the early 1950s.
Left: An early 1950s photograph taken in the public hall, now the Corn Exchange.
Top left: The founder, Richard Bamber with one of the original staff.

Preparing Preston's children for a brighter future

In 1954 a group of Catholic businessmen felt the need for an independent school for Catholic boys to prepare them for entry into the Preston Catholic College and other Catholic public schools.

In May 1955 forty boys under ten were enrolled to form St Pius X School. Premises were a large house in Moor Park Avenue. Bishop Pearson became Chairman of the school governors and the founder headmaster was Mr J G Georgeson. Miss Josie Pearson was the founder teacher.

Two moves followed, first to a wing of St Vincent's School and later to the present premises at Oak House. Here it became an established school,

Above: Form 5 pupils in 1968 outside Oak House with the Headmaster, Mr. G. Georgeson.
Left: Parents building an adventure playground alongside Oak House in 1963.
Below: A few of the first St. Pius boys in 1957, chatting with the founder, Bishop Pearson and Headmaster, Mr. Georgeson.

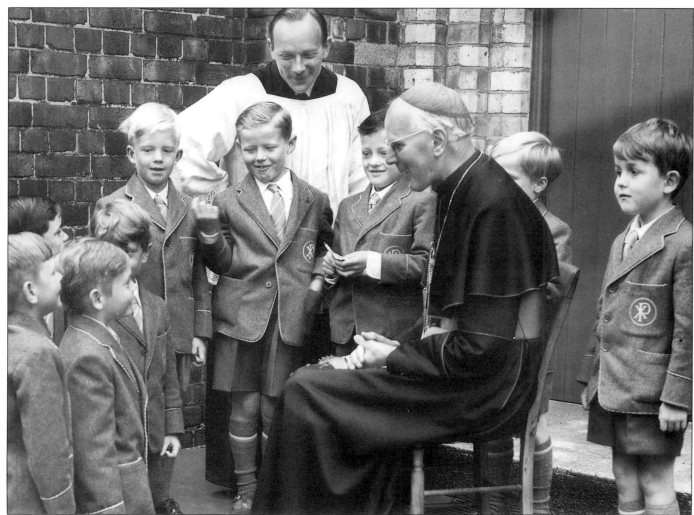

St. Pius X has a tradition of academic excellence and is committed to nurturing and enhancing each child's academic potential. The school seeks to treat and recognise the children as individuals, developing their talents through a broad range of curricular and extra-curricular activities, the aim being to prepare them thoroughly for their transition to senior school at the age of eleven.

The establishment is noted for its happy, caring environment. Socially, much emphasis is placed upon developing the children's characters. Good manners, politeness and deference to authority are insisted upon at all times.

Above left: The 1998 Boys & Girls Sportshall Athletics champions.
Top: A whole school photograph taken in 1983. The staff from left are Mrs. P. Parker, Miss B. Banks, Miss P. Fairhurst, Mr. M. Dwyer (Headmaster), Mrs. M. Holden, Mrs. S. Wildsmith and Mr. A. Lees.
Below: Oak House as it is today showing the new Junior block with tennis courts to the right.

recognised by the Department of Education & Science, and numbers swelled to 150.

Spare places were offered to non-Catholics and today children of many denominations attend the school.

It was in April 1972 that the first nine girls were enrolled. A kindergarten department was opened in 1982 and the school is now fully co-educational with an average pupil roll of 320.

On the retirement of Mr Georgeson in 1975, Mr M J Robbins became headmaster until his move to the south in 1980. He was followed by Mr. M. Dwyer (1981 - 1986). Miss Bridgeen Banks then became Headmistress from 1986 to the present day.

The school, which is owned by CPS (Preston) Ltd, is a non-profit-making charitable trust administered by a board of governors, and is a member of the Incorporated Association of Preparatory Schools and Independent Schools Information Service.

Preston College - looking to the future

Preston College was formed in September 1974 from the amalgamation of the Preston Sixth Form College, the Day College at Alston Hall, certain courses at Glovers Court Day College and the non-advanced courses at the former Harris College, Preston (which went on to become Preston Polytechnic in 1974).

The first phase of the new College buildings at St. Vincent's Road, Fulwood was fully operational in January 1976 and provided four teaching blocks for Science and Humanities courses. The occupation of phase two, a library and general teaching block began in May 1977. The overall site programme was planned by the Borough Architect of Preston.

Recognising the advancing technology of the world, the College offered a diverse range of courses for 16 to 19 year olds, including business studies, Engineering Science and electrical engineering.

"PRESTON COLLEGE WAS THE AMALGAMATION OF FOUR DIFFERENT COLLEGES"

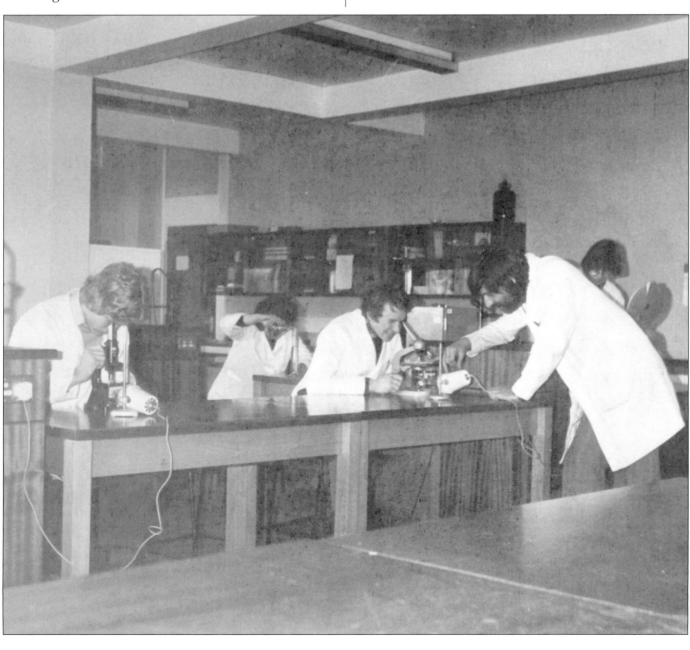

This was in the days before home computers and the internet. Nowadays, The College offers no less than thee courses in computing as well as a wide variety of other courses including languages and sciences.

Preston College attracts some of the more gifted students because it understands how important it is to create opportunities to stretch even the most able. More than half of all subjects taught at A Level are available at the College as well as the opportunity to grow even further with lecturers who are able to develop them to Oxbridge level.

In 1997 Preston College was one of the top ten further education colleges nationally for UCAS score per candidate. The quality of the teaching staff is unrivalled, over the last five years Preston College students have attained among the top five marks in the country for their chosen subject.

The size of the College and the breath of study offered mean that students have access to opportunities unparalleled in the area.

Above: The College as it appeared in the 1970s. **Left:** *Park School, one of the College's buildings.*

Accounting for the needs of local people for almost 130 years

At the turn of the century, Preston was a thriving commercial town. Its prosperity had been built to a large extent on the cotton industry and the inventions of Richard Arkwright, Preston's most famous son. Other forms of industry included iron and brass foundries, engineering works and shipbuilding whilst the commercial base of the town was extended with the development of Preston Docks.

The professional firms in the town were centred mainly on the Winckley Square area and it was there in 1869 that William Francis Moore began practising as an accountant, opening an office at 9 Chapel Street. After some years his two sons

joined him and business grew. However the growth proved a problem and the business was amicably wound up. Mr Moore senior then offered a partnership to his chief clerk Robert Edwin Smalley who had been apprenticed to Mr Moore as an office boy in 1880. So, on January 1st 1892 the firm of Moore & Smalley was established.

Mr Smalley took over several of Mr Moore's duties and soon became the dominant force in the firm. He amended the partnership agreement, giving himself an increase in salary dependent on the firm's annual profits exceeding £800. In 1900 William Moore was taken ill at work and died at the age of 77, leaving Robert Smalley as senior partner.

The firm expanded under Mr Smalley. In 1908 he took into partnership Hugh Southworth and Thomas Bailey who had been with the firm 17 and 11 years respectively. This partnership was a strong one. Many of the clients for whom the firm acted in the early days remain so today.

1869
William Francis Moore founded business
|
Joined by sons who later dissolved partnership
|
January 1892
Robert Edwin Smalley became partner
|
1900
WF Moore died leaving Robert Smalley as sole partner
|
1908
Hugh Southworth and Thomas Bailey became partners
|
Late 1930s
Hugh Southworth retired
|
March 1944
John Donaldson and Stanley Maxwell became partners
|
1947
Thomas Bailey and Robert Smalley died
|
1950
Hugh Southworth's son, also called Hugh joined as partner
|
1975
A merger with Titus, Thorp & Ainsworth took place
|
1986
A merger with Thornton Baker took place

*Above: Robert Smalley, who joined the firm in 1892 after working as an office boy for twelve years. **Top left:** William Francis Moore, founded the firm in 1869. **Left:** The firm's chronology. **Facing page, top:** Invitation to vote for R E Smalley as Borough Auditor. **Facing page, bottom:** Robert Smalley's acceptance as partner.*

Borough Auditors' Election.

Thursday Next, March 1st, 1894.

The favour of your
Vote and Interest
is respectfully solicited on behalf of

R. E. SMALLEY,

Who is at the present time one of the Borough
Auditors and seeks re-election

**The Poll opens at 8 in the Morning
and closes at 8 at night.**

**All Electors vote at the PUBLIC HALL,
Lune Street, on Thursday, Mar. 1st.**

Please mark your Ballot Paper in the third
square as shown below :—

1	COCKER	
2	HINDLE	
3	**SMALLEY**	X
4	THORP	

R. SEED, PRINTER, 12, LUNE STREET, PRESTON.
[TURN OVER.

On New Years Day Thomas Bailey died suddenly having been a partner for 38 years. Later the same month Mr Smalley died at the age of 79. He had been with the firm for more than 60 years, 55 as an active partner. A lengthy obituary in the Lancashire Daily Post listed Mr Smalley's professional achievements and remembered him as a keen sportsman who had kept goal for both Everton and Preston North End, eventually becoming a director of the latter.

John Donaldson and Stanley Maxwell continued the name of Moore & Smalley and links with the past were strengthened when, in 1950, Hugh Southworth came into the partnership where his father had been for many years.

A notable first for the firm occurred in 1955 when William Carrington was elected President of the Institute of Chartered Accountants in England & Wales. He had been articled with Moore & Smalley in the 20s and was the first 'son' of the firm to achieve such high office.

Mr Moore was heavily involved with philanthropic institutions and acted for E H Booth & Company Ltd, whilst Mr Smalley was a trustee of the Shepherd Street Mission.

Another link that endures is with Vernon-Carus Ltd of Penwortham. Moore & Smalley were the auditors of Vernon & Company Ltd for many years. Vernon-Carus Ltd was formed in 1969, following the merger of Vernon & Company Ltd with Alexander Carus & Sons Ltd and Moore & Smalley continue to act for the company today. One client that got away was the company that grew into Leyland Motors.

There were few changes in the partnership for many years. Mr Southworth retired, dying in 1943. In March 1944 John Donaldson and Stanley Maxwell, both longstanding employees of the practice, were admitted to partnership. The start of 1947 brought two major blows to Moore & Smalley.

MOORE & SMALLEY,
CHARTERED ACCOUNTANTS
TELEPHONE Nº 290

9. Chapel Street,
Preston.

December 1908

Dear Sir,

I beg to inform you that I have taken into partnership Mr Hugh Southworth and Mr Thomas Henry Bailey both of whom are Associates of the Institute of Chartered Accountants and have been connected with this firm for 17 years and 11 years respectively

The business will be carried on under the same style as heretofore

Yours truly
R. E. Smalley

Over the years there were further changes in the partnership. Then 1975 brought the most significant change to the firm since its inception. It joined forces with Titus, Thorp & Ainsworth, Chartered Accountants. The latter firm was prominent in the Preston area and also had strong links with the South Lakeland area. There had been a tenuous link between the two firms in 1894 when Titus Thorp challenged Robert Smalley for the post of Borough Auditor.

Another major change had occurred in 1986 when the Preston and Fylde offices of the then Thornton Baker merged with Moore & Smalley. One of the effects of this amalgamation was to expand the operations of the firm to include an office in Adelaide Street, Fleetwood and, briefly, Blackpool.

MOORE & SMALLEY
CHARTERED ACCOUNTANTS

ROBERT E. SMALLEY, F.C.A.
THOMAS H. BAILEY, F.C.A.
JOHN DONALDSON, A.C.A., A.S.A.A.
STANLEY T. MAXWELL, A.C.A.

9 CHAPEL STREET,
PRESTON.

July, 1944.

TELEPHONE NO. 5296 (TWO LINES)

Messrs. Moore & Smalley beg to announce that MR. JOHN DONALDSON, A.C.A., A.S.A.A., and MR. STANLEY THORBURN MAXWELL, A.C.A., both of whom have been with the Firm for many years have, as from 31st March, been admitted as Partners.

The practice will continue to be carried on under the same name as heretofore.

The main base of Moore & Smalley has always been Preston and specifically the Winckley Square area. The offices at Chapel Street were home to the firm from when William Moore first set up in practice in 1869 to 1966 and when the firm eventually moved it was only to premises across the road. The stay there was comparatively brief before the last move in 1977 to the Royal Insurance Offices at 9, Winckley Square.

The centenary of Moore & Smalley was celebrated in 1992 the year that Preston celebrated the Guild Merchant. Further expansion of the services provided took place in 1996 with the formation of financial planning and forensic accounting divisions to complement the existing specialist departments providing taxation and computer services.

Computerisation now extends to every area of the firm's operations.

The firm are proud to be sponsors of the Moore & Smalley Palace Shield cricket competition, founded in 1902, and have many links with charities in the Preston and Flyde area.

The small practice founded by William Moore all those years ago has now grown into the largest Preston-based firm of chartered accountants. All those associated with Moore & Smalley take great pride in the fact that the name of the firm has endured for over 100 years.

There have been many changes over its lifetime and the next century will doubtless bring many more. However the firm is confident of maintaining its proud reputation within the business community of Preston and beyond.

Above: The Moore & Smalley Palace Shield.
Above left: John Donaldson's and Stanley Maxwell's acceptance as partners in 1944. Below: The current partners at the Preston office of Moore & Smalley.

R Baron Ltd - a century of craftsmanship

The exact date that R Baron was founded is unknown but records show that it became a limited company in 1918. In the beginning Robert Baron carried out domestic repairs and coffin making in Deepdale, walking miles to each job and trundling a handcart of tools over the cobbles.

The firm moved to Peel Hall Street at the beginning of the first war. At the end of the second war Robert Baron handed over management to his two sons, William Albert and Robert Roland, the latter being the father of the current managing director, Robert John Baron. The original Robert was self taught but he insisted that his sons received the best available training at the Harris Technical College.

Soon the Peel Hall Street works had a two storey workshop as the firm grew steadily, concentrating on maintenance and retail shop fitting. When the demand for shop fitting services grew Barons seized the advantage.

A turning point came when Marks & Spencer plc gave Barons a small but urgent repair job. It was done in exemplary fashion and led to M&S becoming one of Barons' valued regular customers. The plumber responsible for this crucial repair was no less than the soon-to-be-famous Tom Finney! Before long the company was appointed regional contractor for M&S plc with responsibility for maintaining seventeen major stores in the region with a watching brief at a further fourteen stores.

Barons fitted out the first Kentucky Fried Chicken restaurant in the UK- in Preston, of course, as well as many other well known organisations such as Preston North End Football Club, several banks, breweries and many high street stores. The firm's work is still predominantly joinery but a plumbing division has been operating since early 1997.

The management believes firmly in 'family business values and judges the company's success by the level of repeat business. Training is a major strength and it is no coincidence that several members of staff who joined the firm as apprentices have stayed on until retirement.

Above and left: Robert Baron, in trademark homburg hat, oversees some local contracts.

A partnership built from pride in the past

When Preston Dock was opened in June 1892 by the Duke of Edinburgh, it had the distinction of being the biggest single dock in the country with a water area of 40 acres.

The Albert Edward Dock 3,200 feet long and 600 feet wide, was equipped to deal with all manner of cargo, ranging from cattle to oil, and saw traffic from Belfast, Dublin, London, Hamburg, Gothenburg and Norway.

The River Ribble had been navigated by small craft since earliest times but the shifting unmarked channel restricted passage to the docks to all but the smallest coastal vessels.

Extensive dredging increased the navigable depth from 16 feet to 22 feet six inches, which had an immediate effect on the number and size of the ships using the port. The dock played its part in both world wars. Between 1939 and 1945 it handled large shipments of food supplies, raw materials and munitions. Before the second war, the dock had operated at a loss of about £35,000 a year which increased to £85,000 before the tide turned in the 1950s.

In 1953 the port paid its way for the first time in sixty years. It continued to flourish, importing 24,000 tonnes of bananas a year by 1958. The trade in citrus fruits and bananas brought an entirely new industry to Preston and made use of the then most modern practice of conveyor belts and electric elevators.

However the dock eventually proved to be the commercial venture which never quite succeeded. It showed the world new ways of handling cargo-containers and 'roll on roll off' -that beat all that

had gone before but later were the cause of its demise. When other ports adopted Preston's methods they stole its trade. The dock ended as it had begun with struggle.

When the deficits reached more than £1 million a year the council decided it had to go. Royal assent was given on July 23rd 1981 and the gates closed for the last time.

The next few years saw the "Riversway Docklands" revitalised by new flats, houses, offices, super-stores, public houses, restaurants, cinema and a 100 berth marina to attract new types of vessel.

By the early 90s it was realised everywhere and locally that public, private and voluntary organisations must work in partnership to achieve results. The Preston Partnership was created in 1994 and later incorporated the neighbouring Borough to

Above: The Maritime '97 Festival which attracted over 100 boats of all types.
Left: Vessels leaving Preston Dock via 'Bullnose'. Facing page: The dock as it appeared at the turn of the century.

partnership to attract £6.6 million of regeneration cash for Deepdale (unlocking 3 to 4 times that amount from other sources) and achieved record levels of Lottery grants per head to support a new outdoor multi-sport complex, football museum, cultural centre, improvements and better utilisation of the town's Guild Hall and Parish Churches, linking the 42 mile Lancaster Canal to the Inland Waterways network and many other schemes. These projects were supported by other initiatives to improve the quality of life of local people - partly by crime prevention measures including a complete closed circuit television system for Preston Town Centre.

Another early aspiration resulted from a trip to Glasgow by many of the inaugural members of the Partnership. Hearing about the benefits of the one off Glasgow Garden Festival - achieved with millions of pounds of Government cash - they asked

become the Preston & South Ribble Partnership. The chief executive was Andrew Harris who had held senior positions in the public and private sectors and a similar partnership post in the Isle of Man when he had commuted from Preston Dock in his ketch 'Amethyst', a sign of the Maritime theme that would later be developed.

The new Partnership aimed to make Preston & South Ribble a place "Where people aspire to live, enjoy working and love visiting". The first priority, however, was to break the local jinx which had prevented any Government regeneration cash or similar funding being attracted to the area. Within three years the new organisation had more than 50 public, private and voluntary member organisations and had worked in

Above: The Sailors' Hornpipe.
Right: The Royal Navy Window Ladder Display which was discontinued after it's appearance at the Preston Maritime Festival.

the new chief executive to suggest a major event that could invigorate the area, raise the profile of the town and be enjoyed by local people and visitors alike. Sensing a public fascination with things Maritime Andrew Harris suggested a Preston Maritime Festival which could make the most of the major but little used facility Preston Dock with the new marina and amenities.

The first Preston Maritime Festival was held in July 1995 with the Royal Navy's Window Ladder Display as the "flagship" event. With contributions from more than 60 organisations the Festival was an instant hit. The Preston Maritime Festival '96 attracted even more visits from sea going and canal boats and attracted the brigantine Zebu which later registered in Preston and entered Tall Ships Races flying the Preston flag.

The Preston Maritime Festival '97 attracted well over 100,000 people and achieved international press coverage. By 1998 the Festival was being organised by Partnership Projects Limited - the company run by Andrew Harris to manage the Preston & South Ribble Partnership.

This annual event became well established and special arrangements were being made in 1998 to build on the Festival as one means of celebrating the New Millennium in the year 2000.

Kent Healthcare - caring for the community

Kent & Son (Homes) Ltd, trading as Kent Healthcare, was established in 1975 by Thomas Kent and his son John.

Thomas Kent served in the RAF during the second war. Later he rose to be Works Manager in an engineering foundry before becoming a newsagent, operating various businesses in Preston, Yorkshire and the Fylde coast.

Meanwhile John Kent attended the Leeds College of Commerce and Harris College, Preston (now the University of Central Lancashire) before joining the family firm in 1965.

When it was decided to change tack to healthcare, the first residential homes the family bought were in Blackpool and Southport. The Sylvester Private Residential Home in Reads Avenue, Blackpool, is still operated by the company, though it would be unrecognisable today by its early residents. The Langdales in Hornby Road, Blackpool was purchased in 1978, but the big jump was the building of Sherwood Lodge in Preston. One of the first luxury purpose built homes in the country, it opened in 1985 and set the pattern for the company's future development. It was much larger than the average home of the day and designed to operate on hotel lines. It offered an entirely new concept of care for the elderly.

from their Preston Head Office.

There are two sources of customers, private ones and those funded wholly or partially by the state via the social services. Everyone has choice of where they would like to live so hard work is involved in ensuring that the company's homes are a first choice. The properties are modern, spacious and homely and offer high quality care that people can trust. The management realises that it is often small details that make the biggest difference.

Further purpose-built nursing and residential homes at Blackpool, Preston and Lancaster have followed. Each one incorporated the lessons learned from the previous one in a continuous drive towards higher standards.

Having a happy, well motivated and caring staff is fundamental to the level of customer service the company aims for. Residential and nursing homes are essentially there to serve the local community in which they are based and good ones put down very firm roots in their areas. The company has deliberately restricted the development of homes to Preston, Blackpool and, recently, Lancaster so that they can monitor the standards of care and service

Recently the company established its own group of independent financial advisers who set up a specialist subsidiary, Healthcare Funding UK Ltd. Now they are able to offer packages to help customers minimise the drain on assets due to the payment of long term care fees. Over half of their customers fund privately and the company wishes to help them protect their assets as far as possible.

The management aims constantly to reinforce its position as first choice among professionals by improving the services, making customers' stays happy and giving their friends and relatives peace of mind and confidence that their loved ones are content.

Currently the company is developing a new 44 bed residential home which will offer service and accommodation to people in the Ingol and Fulwood areas of Preston. It now has 23 years' experience in the Private Residential and Nursing Homes sector and 15 years' experience in designing new homes which provide a warm and homely environment.

*Above: Indoor games. **Left:** The official opening ceremony in April 1990. **Left to right:** Marion Fogarty (matron at the time), Rt. Hon. David Waddington M.P. (Home Secretary) and John Kent of Kent Healthcare. **Facing page, top right:** Preston Guild Party for Lodge and Court residents. **Facing page, top left:** Thomas Kent. **Facing page, bottom:** Sherwood Court.*

Independent financial advice for almost twenty years

Taylor Patterson Associates Limited was established in 1979 by the founders, Nigel Taylor and John Patterson to provide specialist advice on pensions and financial services. Both had considerable experience to offer following many years as directors of a major firm of insurance brokers and independent financial advisers.

The Company was initially set up in rented premises equipped with just two typewriters and a photo-copying machine.

The business expanded over the next eight years with two separate moves to larger rented premises around Winckley Square in Preston.

In 1987 the Company purchased premises at 25B Winckley Square. This building had previously

Above: This photograph dates from when the Company took over the premises at 25B, Winckley Square. It shows a view of the inside.

Below: This picture shows Lanson House, Winckley Gardens before the sign was placed above the doorway.

been part of the Catholic College complex around Winckley Square and had been empty for a number of years. Substantial renovation was carried out to bring this up to a modern office standard.

Again the Company outgrew these premises and acquired the current premises of Lanson House, Winckley Gardens in Mount Street, Preston.

Today, Taylor Patterson Financial Services Group is an independent financial adviser providing a wide range of professional services to clients throughout the UK, ranging from private individuals to Public Limited Companies.

The Company specialises in the management of Small Self Administered Schemes for director controlled limited companies, Self Invested Personal Pensions for private individuals and

provides a full range of administration and technical services, covering all aspects of employee benefit.

Included within the group is Taylor Patterson Trustee Services Ltd, providing independent trusteeship for employee benefit schemes and Taylor Patterson Insurance Services Ltd, managing corporate and private general insurance.

Since the establishment of Taylor Patterson Associates Ltd in June 1979, the Company has acquired a reputation for professional advice and is one of the leading financial services groups in the North of England. Considerable investment in both people and technology is constantly being made to extend and improve these services for the future.

Below: Lanson House today.

"TODAY, THE COMPANY HAS A RANGE OF CLIENTS THROUGHOUT THE UK"

Members of the cast of the Merrie England show staged in Avenham Park in 1952

ACKNOWLEDGMENTS

LANCASHIRE COUNTY LIBRARY: HARRIS LIBRARY

PETER G REED

© TRUE NORTH HOLDINGS

ISBN 1 900 463 17 2